# WATER SKIING
## The Skills of the Game

# Water Skiing
## The Skills of the Game

### JOHN WEST

THE CROWOOD PRESS

First published in 1989 by
The Crowood Press
Ramsbury, Marlborough
Wiltshire SN8 2HE

British Library Cataloguing in Publication Data

West, John
    Water skiing:the skills of the game.
    1. Water skiing. Manuals
    I. Title
    797.3'5

    ISBN 1-85223-138-6

**Dedicated to Gillian**

**Acknowledgements**

All line-drawings except for Chapter 2 by Ursula Mathews.
All photographs courtesy of Stanley Searle, except cover photograph
and Figs 43, 50-3, 71, 83-4, 91, 95-100, 102-3 by Gavin Newman.
The author would like to thank Gary Shipman and the British Water Ski
Federation for all their support.

Typeset by Alacrity Phototypesetters
Banwell Castle, Weston-super-Mare
Printed in Great Britain by The Bath Press

# Contents

Introduction 7

1 History 9

2 Getting Ready to Ski 10

3 Starting on Two Skis 12

4 Mono Skiing 26

5 An Introduction to Slalom Skiing 41

6 The Slalom Course 53

7 Trick Skiing 60

8 Jumping 80

9 Barefoot 91

10 Competitive Water Skiing 94

11 Equipment 100

Appendix A 105

Appendix B 106

Glossary 107

Index 109

John West began water skiing in 1971 and has since enjoyed a distinguished career both as a junior, winning the slalom event at the European Junior Championships in 1979, and as a member of the British Senior Team, competing from 1979 to 1981.

He began coaching at Ruislip, the home of British water skiing, before going on to coach the Greek, Danish and Irish national teams. In 1987 he was appointed British National Coach.

John West is currently Staff Coach to the British Water Ski Federation and is actively involved in coaching the British Junior Team.

John West first came to the notice of the National Coach – the late David Nations – in 1972, when only 12 years old, and under David's guidance became European Junior Slalom Champion in 1979. John was a regular member of the British Senior Team until 1981 when he took up coaching. In 1987 he became British Junior Team Captain and National Coach to the British Water Ski Federation.

I cannot think of a better qualified person to help teach the correct skills and techniques for beginners right through to more advanced skiers. This superb book displays the sort of professional approach to coaching needed to help advance our rapidly-growing sport in a safe and correct manner.

**Gary Shipman**
*Coaching Officer*
*British Water Ski Federation*

# Introduction

My aim in this book is to provide a helpful and concise insight into the sport of water skiing. Water skiing comprises a whole range of activities and is a sport open to all the family at any age. I hope this book will demonstrate that water skiing offers more than a quick dip in the Mediterranean on a summer holiday.

Teaching yourself any sport relies on your ability to learn from your mistakes. It is possible to identify problems at an early stage by continually experimenting with position, weight distribution and timing, and noticing how they affect your skiing. An awareness of these factors and their combination during a manoeuvre enables you to make an objective assessment of what went wrong. Remember, it is just as important to look for what went right, and to try and reproduce the correct combination. The ability to recognise a particular problem, to understand how it occurred and what cor-

rective action needs to be taken is the key to rapid progress. Throughout this book each technique and the underlying theory is explained and where possible the skill is broken down into a series of simple steps. Areas where problems are likely to arise are highlighted and are accompanied by suggestions on how to overcome them.

Inevitably, achieving success requires a disciplined approach coupled with determination and knowledge of the principles involved. This book is designed to make the transition from novice to accomplished skier easier.

The following chapters progress from basic water skiing on two skis to intermediate-level slalom tricks, jump and barefoot. It is important to remember at every stage that good preparation and self-discipline will improve your success rate and hence increase your enjoyment of the sport.

# 1 History

## ORIGINS

Water skiing, or aquaplaning as it was known, first appeared in the early 1900s. The origins of aquaplaning are unclear, but one story is that it came to being during a swim in the Pacific after a fishing trip. On leaving for home, one of the party did not want to get out of the water. The captain, not wanting to be delayed, attached a rope to the lid of a fish box and threw it overboard so that the swimmer could hold on to it whilst being dragged home. It was not long before the swimmer was standing on the board and calling for another line to be thrown for him to hold on to. The idea caught the imagination of many people and quickly developed so that various tricks and manoeuvres came to be performed.

## DEVELOPMENT OF THE SPORT

As the sport progressed, the aquaplanes became more refined and were even manufactured commercially. The aquaplane was essentially a board about 2–3m (6.5–10ft) long and 1m (3ft) wide with a rope tied to the front. The aquaplaner held on to a supporting rope which was attached to the tip of the board. In this way it was possible to stand up and use body-weight to control the board.

The main limitation in the early days was the speed of the motor launch which was restricted to about 20kph (12mph). With time, the skills of the aquaplaners grew as the performance of the boats improved. To assist with manoeuvrability, the aquaplane was split into two long planks with each 'ski' tied to the boat. A rope attached to the tips with a handle for the 'skier' to hold on to was still the main form of control. The feet were tied to the skis by rubber bands and skegs were fitted to the bottom to assist with stability. Shortly after progressing from the single board on to two skis the tow rope was removed from the tips of the skis and held by the skier.

Both sides of the Atlantic claim to have been the first to 'do it' on two skis, but the birth of water skiing as we know it today truly occurred around 1930.

# 2 Getting Ready to Ski

## PHYSICAL PREPARATION

Skiing is a physical sport and a one hundred per cent effort will tire even the best of skiers after a few minutes. The 'water time' is small compared to the time spent on land so a good preparation before going on to the water will help you to get the best from your skiing.

## Warming-up Exercises

Warming up prior to skiing will improve performance and reduce the risk of injury. Certainly, if you are expecting to push yourself to the limit of your skiing ability it is a good idea to prepare your body for the stress and strain involved in a hard skiing work-out. This is especially true when skiing in cool water. A few minutes' jogging or stretching is adequate preparation for most of the activities outlined in this book. The following is a list of suggested exercises beneficial to the skier:

1. *Neck.* Sitting or standing, slowly rotate your head around in a full circle, changing direction after every rotation.

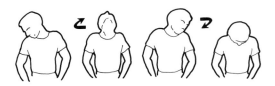

*Fig 1   Neck.*

2. *Shoulders and chest.* Standing upright with your hands on your head, bend sideways at the waist, keeping your back straight. To increase the stretching effect hold your elbows in your hands.

*Fig 2   Shoulders and chest.*

3. *Arms, shoulders and chest.* Standing upright, extend your arms above your head, twisting them inwards so that the palms are together. Keeping your arms straight, slowly stretch them upwards and backwards, holding the stretched position for several seconds.

*Fig 3   Arms, shoulders and chest.*

4. *Arms and shoulders*. Standing or sitting, hold the elbow of one arm with the hand of the other above your head. Pull your elbow across the back of your head whilst holding the hand of that arm down.

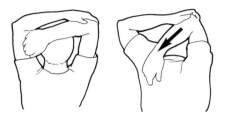

*Fig 4   Arms and shoulders.*

5. *Hamstrings*.   Sitting on the floor, extend one leg straight in front and pull the foot of the other leg up so that the sole is touching the inside of the thigh. Keeping your head up and your back straight, stretch forwards towards the foot of the extended leg. Hold this position for several seconds and then try with the other leg.

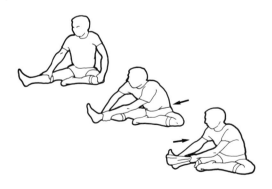

*Fig 5   Hamstrings.*

6. *Lower back*.   Lying on your back with your hands behind your head, bend your knees and touch the floor with your elbows. By tightening the stomach and buttock muscles the lower back will flatten and exert pressure on the floor. Hold the tension for ten seconds.

*Fig 6   Lower back.*

7. *Hips and inner thighs*.   Sit on the floor with your legs straight and spread in front of you. Slowly bend forward and stretch towards each foot alternately, holding the stretched position for several seconds.

*Fig 7   Hips.*

# MENTAL PREPARATION

Preparing yourself mentally involves planning the session by considering the water conditions and the success or failure of the last session. Once you have decided on a plan of action discuss it with the boat driver or coach prior to getting into the water. Good communication between you and the boat means that all the information you need may be conveyed by a few key words or hand signals.

# 3   Starting on Two Skis

The first attempts at most sports may prove to be all too embarrassing. This is especially true of water skiing as the distinction between success and failure is so marked. However, it is comforting to know that almost everyone takes several attempts to get out of the water on their first session and that if you persevere until you succeed you will be rewarded with a unique experience.

## DRY LAND LESSON

Before venturing on to the water practise on dry land. Becoming familiar with the equipment and technique by watching other skiers and practising the basic movements will improve your chances of success.

For the dry land lesson you will need a rope and handle and someone to assist. The object is to practise the movements involved in starting from the water. To begin, sit on the ground and pull your knees up to your chest. Hold the handle in a palms-down grip at arm's length. The ideal position is shown in Fig 9, and is a close approximation to the actual position in the water. To give a feeling of security and to help with stability in the water, gently squeeze your knees together between your arms, remembering that your arms should be straight.

The next step is to practise standing up.

Fig 8   Palms-down grip.

Fig 9    The ideal start position.

Fig 10    Trying to pull yourself up can be a disappointing experience.

## Starting on Two Skis

Hold the handle in the start position and get someone, preferably someone with some skiing experience, to pull the rope. The secret is to relax and let whoever is pulling the rope do all the work. Trying to pull yourself up will not work. Fig 10 shows the typical reaction of a skier trying to pull on the rope. Problems of this type will always show up at this stage and must be ironed out before continuing. Practising the start on dry land gives a good indication of the mistakes you are likely to make and provides you with the ideal opportunity to ensure that faults do not persist.

As the rope starts to pull, stand up slowly as in the sequence shown in Figs 11–13. In the final position you should be looking straight ahead with your weight on the balls of your feet. Notice that the upper body moves very little, the legs are never fully extended and the arms remain straight. The importance of keeping the arms straight needs to be emphasised as pulling with the arms is usually accompanied by upper body movement leading, very often, to a fall backwards. Likewise, the beginner is not encouraged to stand up too much on the first few attempts as this may have a similar effect. Although the final position shown in the sequence is not the best, it is the most stable for beginners and you should stay in this position until you have control over the skis.

Figs 11-13 The start sequence on dry land. As the rope starts to pull, make sure that your weight is on the balls of your feet. Slowly stand up but do not fully extend your legs.

Fig 12

Fig 13

Fig 14  The correct skiing position.

16

## Key Points to Remember

1.   Don't stand up too quickly. All movement should be steady and smooth to ensure that balance is maintained.
2.   Never fully extend your legs.
3.   Keep your arms straight.

This routine should be practised as many times as necessary until it is possible to go from the start position to the final position in one fluid movement, finishing with your weight on the balls of your feet.
  Once you are fully satisfied with this stage then you may try the correct skiing position. The reason for leaving this until last is that standing up into this position immediately often leads to a loss of balance. Remaining in the position shown in Fig 13 until stable, straighten your back slowly until the correct skiing position is assumed (*see* Fig 14). This will ensure that balance is maintained.

## POSITION CHECK-LIST

From the feet upwards:

1)   Skis shoulder-width apart.
2)   Equal weight on both feet.
3)   Weight on balls of feet.
4)   Knees bent and flexible.
5)   Back straight.
6)   Arms straight.
7)   Head up.

## GETTING INTO THE WATER

The first thing that you need is a life-jacket. No matter how good a swimmer you are, this item is indispensable – falling at speed is potentially dangerous and a good quality life-jacket provides valuable protection as well as being helpful when putting the skis on in the water.

*Fig 15   Wet the skis to ensure a good fit.*

Fig 16 Sit down to one side on the jetty and swing the skis over the edge.

Fig 17 Paddle slowly with your free arm and pull your knees up to your chest to get into position.

Before putting the skis on, dip them in the water to wet the bindings. This makes it easier to slip them on and ensures a good fit. If you are getting into the water from a jetty, put the skis on whilst standing up. Once the skis are on, sit down to one side and swing the skis over the edge. From this position it is easy to slide into the water.

At this point the reason for the dry land lesson becomes apparent. The skis may not behave in the way that you expected and the result may be that you start to flounder. Getting into the start position and paddling gently with your arms to maintain your position will correct the situation. If in the worst case you find that you are face down, roll on to your back.

## FIRST ATTEMPTS

Once you are stable in the water the next step is to get the skis parallel and shoulder-width apart with the tips just showing out of the water. Check that your knees are up to your chest and your arms are straight. When the rope is taut and you are satisfied with your position, signal to the driver that you are ready to go. Remember, the start from the water is similar to the one you practised on dry land. Initially, as the boat starts to pull there appears to be a lot of drag and spray. Trying to pull yourself up must be avoided as it only increases the drag and alters the body position. Let the boat do all the work and stand up slowly, remembering not to fully

*Fig 18 As the rope tightens, maintain your position.*

*Fig 19 Once up, slowly straighten your back.*

extend your legs. Don't straighten your back until you have control over the skis.

If all goes well you will be up and skiing. However, water skiing is about balance and it may take a few attempts to find the correct position. Once up, resist the temptation to pull on the rope to adjust your position.

## Falling

Whenever you have fallen but have not injured yourself, put your arm in the air to signal to the driver that you are all right.

If you fall and keep your skis on you are lucky. More often than not the skis will come

| Fault | Cause |
|---|---|
| 1. Falling backwards | a) Pulling on the arms <br> b) Straightening the back too soon <br> c) Leaning too far back at the start |
| 2. Falling sideways | a) Being off balance at the start <br> b) Pushing unequally with your legs |
| 3. Falling forwards | a) Straightening your legs too quickly <br> b) Leaning too far forwards at the start |
| 4. Skis opening | a) Skis too far apart at the start <br> b) Pushing unequally with the legs |
| 5. Being unable to stand up | a) Weight on your heels |

off and this poses the problem of putting them on in the water. This may be more difficult than at first appears. The best approach is to prepare the ski by holding it vertically in the water and opening the binding with both hands. Then, in one movement, bend your knee up to your chest, put your toes into the binding and pull hard with your arms. A quick, single movement is required to reduce the chance of losing your balance. It is fruitless to continue trying to put the skis on if you are lying on your side or face down in the water.

# CROSSING THE WAKE

To turn the skis, lean in the direction that you want to go. If you want to ski to the right then lean to the right and put more weight on the left ski. To ski to the left, lean to the left and exert pressure on the right ski. The more that you lean and exert pressure on the ski the more the ski will turn and the faster you will approach the wake. Before crossing the wake practise skiing from side to side directly behind the boat. This will give you the opportunity to feel how the skis behave and gain confidence. To cross the wake just continue to lean in the direction you wish to go whilst maintaining position. Once you

have crossed the top of the wake you are effectively skiing downhill and the skis will start to accelerate. If your weight is not on the balls of your feet the skis will slide away.

Ideally, you should approach the wake at an angle and at speed, to avoid the skis getting caught in the turbulence at the crest. This may present some problems as the shock of hitting the wake is greater when crossing at speed. To reduce the effect of the wake, bend your knees to absorb the shock. Remember, the faster you go through the wake the faster you will have to bend your knees. Sometimes it helps to anticipate the wake by thinking about flexing your knees on the approach. At all times keep a strong upper body, trying not to bend at the waist.

# DRY START (JETTY)

The dry start enables you to start skiing without getting wet and is particularly useful on cold days.

Sit on the edge of the jetty facing the direction of the boat. Don't sit too close to the edge of the jetty as this may affect your balance. The start position is shown in Fig 21.

| Fault | Cause |
|---|---|
| 1. Falling backwards | a) Too much weight on your heels as you pass over the crest of the wake which in turn is caused by leaning too far back to compensate for the extra pull on the rope. |
| | Keeping your weight on the balls of your feet will ensure that correct balance is maintained. |
| 2. Being unable to cross the wake | a) Not leaning enough. |
| | One way of overcoming this problem is to ski from side to side behind the boat, building up sufficient momentum to carry you over the wake. |

# Starting on Two Skis

Fig 20 *Maintain position when crossing the wake.*

*Fig 21   Starting from the jetty.*

There should be some slack in the rope as the boat starts to accelerate, the amount of which depends upon the weight of the skier and the pulling power of the boat. The chances of success depend very much on the boat driving. Too fast a pull caused by too much slack will generally result in the skier being pulled head first into the water. Too slow, that is not enough slack, and the skier will sink.

Let's assume that the pull is correct. When the slack rope takes up, absorb the pull with your arms, trying not to let them reach full extension. As you are pulled off the jetty it is important to bend your knees. This lowers your centre of gravity and puts you in a stronger position to take the pull.

## Key Points to Remember

1.  Lean back.
2.  Keep your arms in.

| Fault | | Cause | |
|---|---|---|---|
| 1. | Falling backwards | a) | Leaning too far back at the start |
| | | b) | Slow pull from the boat |
| 2. | Falling forwards | a) | Leaning too far forward at the start |
| | | b) | Not resisting the pull with your arms |
| | | c) | Stiff legs |
| | | d) | Fast pull from the boat |

## Starting on Two Skis

Fig 22 Bend your knees and use your arms to absorb the pull.

# DRIVING TIPS

With beginners, boat driving becomes an important factor in the success or failure of the skier. A knowledge of the standard of the skier and what he or she intends to do is vital. For complete beginners a slow, smooth pull out of the water is required, making sure that the boat does not race away once it is on the plane. A speed of approximately 30kph (18mph) is sufficient for the average person, depending on their weight. Once the skier appears to be in control the speed may gradually be increased to about 40kph (24mph).

The boat path should consist of straight runs with long, wide turns. It is a good idea occasionally to look at the skier during the turn to see if he or she is having any difficulty.

If the skier is starting to swing out towards the boat's wake during the turn, reduce the speed of the boat to bring him or her back into the centre of the wake. Similarly, if the skier is drifting to the inside of the turn and sinking, increase the speed to keep him or her afloat and again bring the skier towards the centre of the wake. By careful control of the boat's speed it is possible to keep skiers who have little control of their skis in the centre of the wake during corners. Once the skier is able to cross the wake and make the turn without difficulty then tighter and faster turns should be made.

If a skier falls, look for any signal that shows he or she is all right. Approach the skier slowly and, if circling, make sure that the rope is passed over the skier's head.

# 4  Mono Skiing

Skiing on one ski is the most common ambition for skiers new to the sport as it opens the door to greater things. Doing it right not only looks good – it feels good too. Fortunately, if you have mastered skiing on two, it is a simple step to progress on to one ski.

The limitations of skiing on two skis arise from not being able to decelerate enough in order to make a quick, controlled turn. The problem becomes particularly acute when crossing the wake at speed and is characterised by slack appearing in the rope during the turn.

The main advantage of skiing on one ski is that it is easier to maintain control of the ski whilst crossing the wake and during the turn.

## LIFTING A SKI

The first thing to decide is which leg you prefer to stand on. This is best discovered by putting all your weight on one ski whilst lifting the other out of the water. Before attempting to lift the ski it is important to start in a good skiing position. However, this time change the grip on the handle. This enables you to hold the rope lower and adds to stability. The full importance of this will become apparent later. Slowly transfer all your weight on to one leg and lift the ski. Lifting the ski up and forward will ensure that the tip is up and completely clear of the spray.

Check if your body position has changed. A common mistake is to break forward at the waist as the ski is lifted. The idea is to transfer the weight slowly in order not to lose your

position or balance. Remember that skiing is a balancing act and any sudden or erratic movements usually result in a fall. Try each leg alternately to find which suits you best. It will be obvious which leg you favour as most people have one leg stronger than the other.

Having chosen the best leg to stand on, practise lifting the ski until it is possible to ski for long periods without losing your balance. In theory, if you are able to ski 100-200m (110–220yd) with the ski out of the water then it is possible to ski on one ski.

Fig 23   The slalom grip.

*Fig 24    Lift the ski up and forward so that it is clear of the spray.*

| Fault | Cause |
|---|---|
| 1.  Falling sideways when lifting ski | a)  Not keeping your weight over the ski when lifting your leg |
| 2.  Ski swerving from side to side | a)  Breaking at the waist |
| | b)  A weak ankle |

If you are satisfied that you can ski for a sufficient period without losing your balance then you are ready to try dropping the ski.

## DROPPING THE SKI

This is the critical stage. The best way to drop a ski is to do it slowly and carefully in order not to lose your balance. Lifting the ski and trying to shake it off can be a 'hit or miss' affair and possibly dangerous. First, loosen the binding so that it will come off easily. Start with equal weight on both feet and push down on your toes to lift your heel out of the binding. Remember, push down on the toes to lever the heel out of the ski. Never lift the heel out of the ski without pushing down on your toes as the tail of the ski will lift and the tip may catch in the water.

When the heel is out of the binding, regain your position and slowly transfer all your weight on to the skiing leg. Keeping the drop ski on the water, slowly let the ski drag behind whilst lifting the heel up and out. The ski should peel off without too much trouble. You need to be this careful to eliminate any excessive movements which may result in a fall.

Fig 25  *Push the toes down to lever the heel up.*

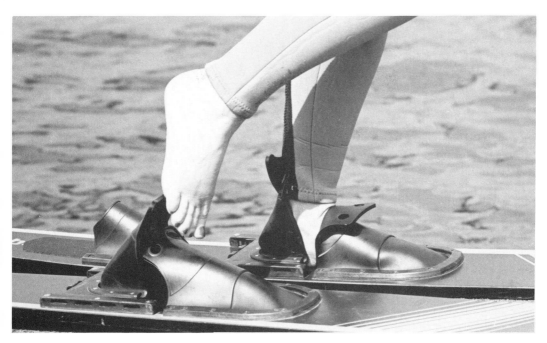

*Fig 26   Let the ski fall behind and slowly lift your foot out of the binding.*

*Fig 27   Rest your toes lightly just behind the front binding.*

Fig 28  *Alternatively, place your foot behind your skiing leg and slide it down using the leg as a guide.*

Once the ski is off, put your toes lightly on the back of the ski. Ideally, this should be done in one continuous movement without looking down at the ski. Place your toes just behind the front binding. At this stage it is not necessary to put your foot in the back binding as this may lead to loss of position. Remember to keep looking ahead. Don't look down at the ski and don't put too much weight on the back of the ski. If you have trouble putting your toes down on the back of the ski you might wish to try an alternative approach. After dropping the ski place your foot directly behind the knee of the skiing leg, holding it there with a little pressure to keep a stable position. Once you are comfortable, slide your foot down to the ski using your skiing leg as a guide.

Once you are stable the next step is gradually to put more weight on the back foot, lowering your heel until it rests firmly on the ski.

| Fault | Cause |
|---|---|
| 1.  Falling backwards | a)  Not having your weight directly over the ski before dropping |
| 2. Ski starts to swerve before you put your foot down on the back of it | a)  Movement at the waist<br>b)  A weak ankle |
| 3. Ski starts to swerve after you put your foot on the back of it | a) and b)   As above<br>c)  Putting too much weight on the back of the ski for someone of your ability |

# POSITION CHECK-LIST

From the feet upwards:

1) Equal weight on both feet.
2) Knees close together and bent.
3) Hips forward.
4) Back straight.
5) Arms low.
6) Head up and looking straight ahead.

## Good Stance

For this position the ideal weight distribution is equal weight on both feet. It is important to remember to keep the back straight and that a good position is one in which a straight line may be drawn between the shoulders, hips and feet. If you feel that you are breaking forward at the waist then it is better to push your hips forward rather than move your shoulders back. Remember to feel how your weight is distributed and readjust it as necessary after each change of position. Only when you are satisfied with your position and are able to have some control over the ski should you consider putting your foot in the back binding. To locate the back binding, slowly move your foot towards the rear of the ski using your toes to feel the ski. Again, slow movements are required to maintain good position. Once the foot is

*Fig 29 The correct position.*

Fig 30 A strong upper body position.

firmly in the binding remember to check the weight distribution and ensure that the heel is fully down.

## The Theory

At this point it is worth considering the theory behind the correct stance.

Equal weight on both feet will cause the ski to ride in its natural attitude, assuming that the ski is set up correctly. Too much weight on the rear foot will make the back of the ski dig into the water and increase the drag. Too much weight on the front foot results in a loss of stability. An indication of the correct weight distribution is given by the spray; looking down at the ski, the spray should start underneath the front foot.

Holding the handle as shown earlier enables the rope to be held lower. Notice how the hips and elbows are close together in Fig 30. This means that the pull is acting at the same height as your centre of gravity and hence leads to the inherent stability of this position. Bending forward at the waist should be avoided at all times as your arms will move away from the body, raising the level of the pull to shoulder height.

The correct position is less tiring and will give you greater control over the ski. Having the elbows resting on the life-jacket makes it easier to keep a strong upper body. A strong position is typified by having a solid upper body and flexible legs.

Fig 31    Bending at the waist leads to loss of
          position.

Fig 32    Turning slowly makes it easier to
          maintain position.

# CROSSING THE WAKE

Crossing the wake is simply a matter of leaning in the direction that you wish to go. The more you lean, the greater the angle through which the ski turns and the faster you will cross the wake. Obviously, crossing the wake on one ski poses problems similar to those experienced on two, but these are easier to cope with on one ski.

You should be aware of your body position and weight distribution at all times during the crossing, remembering to check them after each change of position.

You will run into difficulties if you bend forwards at the waist by letting your hips fall behind during the pull, and again if you do so when crossing the wake. These faults will result in a transferral of the pull to shoulder height and may be sufficient to pull you over the front of the ski, especially when coupled with the slowing down of the ski as you pass through the wake. Try to maintain a strong

upper body positon at all times by pushing your knees and hips forwards rather than leaning back with your shoulders.

During the wake crossing it is important to bend your knees and to ensure that you are fully prepared it is a good idea to anticipate the wake by starting to flex your knees before you reach it.

A less common problem encountered when crossing the wake is that of falling sideways. This is due to the ski remaining flat on the water during the lean as the ski will only turn if it is on its edge. Keep your ankle firm so that the ski will go on its edge as you lean.

The best way to approach the wake crossing is to go slowly at first, concentrating on maintaining position and keeping the ski on edge and skiing only a few metres outside the wake before returning. If you go too far out too early then it is likely that you will build up too much speed and run into difficulties at the wake. Turn slowly and cut towards the wake gently at first, then progressively lean more so that you are leaning the hardest as you pass through the wake. This will ensure that the ski is on edge, enabling you to maintain a strong position.

## Key Points to Remember

1. Maintain a strong upper body position. Don't bend forwards.
2. Bend your knees as you cross the wake. Make sure that you flex sufficiently and that as you cross the wake with more speed, you bend your knees faster.
3. Keep the ski on edge as you pass through the wake. Crossing the wake on a flat ski will cause the ski to ride over the wake rather than cut through it. Keeping the ski on edge will reduce the effect of the wake, making it easier to control.

## START METHODS

## Deep Water Start on One

After picking up the drop ski a few times it is a good idea to learn the deep water start on one. Unfortunately, this proves difficult for the majority of skiers in the initial stages as the techique takes several attempts to perfect.

There are two methods of starting, both of which should be tried depending on the restrictions imposed by the boat. The preferred method is starting with both feet in the bindings. This is easier but requires a stronger boat engine as the drag is greater. The second method is that of starting with only one foot in the bindings with the other trailing behind, and requires less pull from the boat.

### Two-Footed Start

Sitting in the water, put both feet firmly in the bindings and pull your knees up to your chest. The tip of the ski should just be showing out of the water and the tail should be kept high so that the ski lies at a shallow angle. If the ski is vertical the drag created will be too much. For left-footed skiers the rope should be on the right of the ski and vice versa for right-footed skiers.

With your arms straight and your knees between them you are ready to go. This position may be difficult to maintain in the water especially before the boat starts to pull so using one hand to balance yourself in the water is a good idea. However, this means that the boat driver has to make sure that you have both hands on the handle before taking off.

Once the rope is taut, you have two hands on the handle and are well-balanced, the boat will start to pull. As this happens, push with both feet in a forwards direction – if you push straight down the drag increases and the ski will sink under your weight. At the same time as you are pushing your legs forward, straighten your back. The actual motion is a simultaneous straightening of the legs and back until a skiing position is achieved.

### One-Footed Start

This method entails starting with only one foot in the ski and leaving the other to trail in the water. The advantage is that there is less drag created, making it more suitable for boats with smaller engines. However, it requires more balance and a stronger skiing leg.

In the water, keep your knee up to your chest with the free leg slightly out to the side to assist with balance. The rope should again

*Fig 33   Deep water start on one with both feet in bindings.*

*Fig 34   Good balance in the water is essential before starting.*

# Mono Skiing

Fig 35 *Push your legs forward and straighten your back until a skiing position is assumed.*

be on the left for right-footed skiers and vice versa for left-footed skiers. As the boat starts to pull, push the ski forwards and straighten your back. The motion is identical to that of a two-footed start except that the rear foot trails in the water. The difficulty arises as you emerge from the water and find that you are skiing with only one foot in the ski. It is important to wait until you are in a reasonable position before trying to locate the rear binding.

## Faults

The same faults and remedies apply equally to both one and two-footed starts although most problems with the one-footed start result either from trying to put the foot in the rear binding too hastily or from a weak skiing leg.

1. *Falling forwards.* This is the most common result on the first few attempts and is usually caused by letting your shoulders be pulled forward instead of straightening your back, or by pushing down with your legs. Pushing directy down will make the ski sink and increase the drag.

2. *Falling over to the side.* This is a more difficult problem to solve as it indicates a loss of balance which may be traced back to the start position, but may also be caused by not pushing the ski in the direction of the boat. As you are being pulled, concentrate on pushing the ski directly towards the boat. If the problem persists and always results in falling the same way then try to rectify it by leaning over in the opposite direction as the boat starts to pull.

Fig 36  Put both hands on the handle before
the rope tightens.

Fig 37  As the rope starts to pull you should
already be moving forwards.

## Scooter Start

This is an extension of the deep water start with one foot in the binding and is in some ways easier. However, it is recommended that a one-footed deep water start is learned first.

Stand knee deep, holding most of the ski out of the water with the tip up. Make sure that you are facing the boat and that the boat is also straight. At this point a little trial and error is required to find out how much slack rope is necessary. If you are unsure then a good starting-point is to hold about two metres of slack. When you are ready, stand in the position described and wait until there is the correct amount of slack. Signal to the driver to go. As the rope starts to take up, anticipate the pull by moving all your body forwards so you have built up a little forward momentum by the time the rope is taut. As the rope tightens, push yourself out on to the ski, using your bent arms to absorb some of the shock. If your timing is good then you will glide effortlessly on to the water. Again, wait until you are stable before locating the rear binding. Bending your skiing leg will assist in keeping a strong position.

| Fault | Cause |
|---|---|
| 1.  Falling forwards or having the rope pulled out of your hands | a)  Too much slack |
|  | b)  Not anticipating the pull correctly |
| 2. Falling forwards or sinking | a)  Not enough slack |
|  | b)  Pushing out too early |

# Mono Skiing

Fig 38   Jump start.

*Fig 39   Keep a strong upper body and the ski forward.*

## Jump Start

This is effectively the same as a scooter start except that you start completely out of the water. Obviously, the closer you are to the water the more it will resemble a scooter start. The usual place to do a jump start is from a jetty, where the water is at least 1.5m (5ft) deep. The same principles apply as the scooter start except that on impact with the water you have to bend your skiing leg to

absorb the shock otherwise the ski will come to a sudden stop. Also, the higher the jetty the faster the pull required to keep you afloat on impact with the water.

## Dry Start (Jetty)

As with the deep water start there are two options, but in this case the one-footed start is the preferred method.

# Mono Skiing

## One-Footed Start

Sit on the edge of the jetty with the ski in front, your shoulders back and arms in. The amount of slack required is about a metre or two and again entails some trial and error by both the skier and the boat driver. It is important that the boat takes off in a straight line and that the skier is directly facing the boat. As the boat pulls, try to avoid your arms being pulled out to full extension as the resulting snatch could pull you off. Bending your skiing leg helps you maintain a strong position.

## Two-Footed Start

Perhaps the most difficult way to start but essential if you are using double boot bindings. The same principles apply as the one-footed start, but it is necessary to lean back more and have more slack rope. Weight on the back foot increases the drag, so a faster pull is required to stop the ski sinking. To compensate for the extra drag keep your shoulders further back.

Fig 40   *Bending your knee on landing will absorb some of the shock.*

| Fault | Cause |
|-------|-------|
| 1.  Falling backwards | a)  Leaning too far back at the start |
| 2.  Falling forwards | a)  Leaning too far forwards |
|  | b)  Not resisting the pull with your arms |
|  | c)  Stiff legs |

# 5 An Introduction to Slalom Skiing

As your ability to cross the wake improves your next objective will be to make a series of connecting turns. Performing controlled turns after a fast wake crossing requires a good understanding of how the ski works and also correct technique. Fortunately, most of the techniques of water skiing may be broken down into a series of simple steps. Once these have been learned it is an easy process to combine them to reach the desired objective. The following techniques must be learned individually to ensure rapid progress.

## PULLING THROUGH THE WAKES

The term 'pull' is a little ambiguous and requires some explanation. Pulling on the rope may be interpreted as using your arms, your back or even your whole body to pull. Thus while in trick skiing only the arms are used, for the slalom your whole body-weight must be used to generate the pull so that, for example when crossing the wake, the more you lean with your body away from the boat the faster you will go because you feel more

Fig 41   Start the pull by turning slowly and leaning gently in order to maintain position.

Fig 42 *As you approach the wake increase the lean so that the pull is greatest as you pass through it.*

Fig 43 *Pull hardest as you pass through the wake.*

of the effect of the boat's pull. What we mean by pulling, therefore, is that you lean over using your weight to exert a force on the rope.

While your position remains the same throughout the pull, your weight distribution on the ski changes. A good position during the pull is vital as the force exerted is such that any minor fault may result in a potentially dangerous fall.

## Technique

The best way to tackle the technique of pulling is to start slowly and build up until you run into difficulties, making any adjustments to your position before continuing the build-up.

Starting behind the boat in the correct position, make sure that your upper body is strong. Cross the wake so that you are 3-4m (3-4yd) outside it. Check your position, and when ready lean slowly towards the wake, being careful not to build up too much speed. About a metre from the wake, increase your lean so that you are feeling the pull of the boat most as you pass through the wake. Continue leaning away from the boat until you are 1-2m (1-2yd) clear of the second wake. Wait 3-4m (3-4yd) outside the wake, readjust your position and repeat the process.

*Fig 44 Perfect equilibrium.*

Pulling hardest as you pass through the wake ensures that the ski will be on its edge. This is important since it allows the ski to cut through the wake, thus reducing its effect. Avoid crossing the wake on a flat ski as this allows the ski to ride over the wake, causing it to jump out of the water. A flat ski at the wake is usually caused by pulling too hard at the beginning of the movement, building up speed and then easing off as you reach the wake. Ideally, you should do the opposite of this by pulling gently at the beginning and progressively pulling harder as you approach the wake. This ensures that the most lean, and therefore the hardest edge, occurs as you pass through the wake. Making sure that the ski is on its edge is important as a flat ski will limit the speed at which you are able to pass through the wake safely.

Concentrating on a strong upper body and preparing for the wake as you approach it are the two important points to remember. The main diffficulty with the former is that it is not always easy to detect your own upper body movement, so if you feel that this area may be suspect, ask the observer in the boat to watch for any movement.

Eventually, it should be possible to pull hard from the beginning of the pull up to 1-2m (1-2yd) the other side of the wake on a continuous cut without loss of position.

During the pull you will have been leaning directly away from the boat. As you lean, the ski turns so that it is always between your centre of weight and the boat. Thus your weight distribution will have changed little because the ski always turns sufficiently to maintain this balance. However, most skiers prefer to have a little more weight on their back foot during the cut.

By now you should be crossing the wake in a good position, ready to try slowing down.

## Key Points to Remember

1. Ensure that your position is correct before pulling.
2. Pull hardest as you pass through the wake.
3. Keep the ski on edge as you pass through the wake.
4. Continue pulling for only 1-2m (1-2yd) the other side of the wake.

| Fault | Cause |
|---|---|
| 1. Falling forwards over the wake | a) Breaking forward during the initial part of the pull.<br>   To remedy, push your hips forward and straighten your back. |
| 2. Ski goes flat just before wake | a) Pulling too hard at the start |
| 3. Ski jumps the wake | a) Flat ski<br>b) Stiff legs |

# DECELERATION (PRE-TURN)

The quality of the turn depends on the speed of the ski at the apex of the turn. To decelerate, a skier stops leaning away from the boat and starts to lean towards it. This causes the ski to turn the other way and slow down.

During the pull an increase in the lean away from the boat will make the ski turn through a greater angle, increasing the pull and therefore the acceleration. Conversely, at the end of the move, if you lean towards the boat the ski will start to turn the other way, thus reducing the pull and allowing the ski to slow down. The more you lean towards the boat the more the ski turns and therefore the more the ski will slow down.

## Incorrect Technique

A common problem is that of going on to a flat ski before initiating the turn. If the ski is flat it is presenting little resistance to the water and is not slowing you down. A typical scenario is that of a skier going on to a flat ski, putting weight on the back foot to increase the drag on the ski, and then exerting full pressure on the tail of the ski to make the turn. Although it is an effective and easy way for beginners to make a turn, the turn will be severely limited by slack rope.

## Correct Technique

Your objective should be to change directly from one edge to the other in a single

*Fig 45   Keep pulling until 2m (2yd) clear of the second wake.*

*Fig 46    Change edges quickly.*

movement. Remember that the rate at which the ski turns also depends on the weight distribution over the ski during the deceleration. By pushing your knees and hence your weight forward as you change edges the ski will turn faster. Be careful not to bend forward at the waist as your weight will be too far forward to cope with the deceleration. Experimentation with weight distribution will give the required rate of turn for the amount of lean.

## Key Points to Remember

1.   Do not go on to a flat ski.
2.   Change edges immediately.
3.   Keep a straight back.
4.   Do not look down.

| Fault | | Cause | |
|---|---|---|---|
| 1. | Slack rope | a) | Flat ski |
| | | b) | Not leaning into the turn sufficiently |
| 2. | Falling sideways | a) | Too much weight on rear foot |
| | | b) | Looking down. |
| 3. | Falling forwards | a) | Too much weight on front foot |
| | | b) | Looking down |

Fig 47 *As the lean towards the boat increases the arms will extend.*

# THE TURN

As the ski passes the apex of the turn it is moving towards the boat and you will feel the pull again. If the turn is smooth, that is the rate of turn is consistent throughout, then the pull of the boat will increase gradually. If, however, the turn is slow at the beginning and sharp at the end then the pull from the boat will be a snatch. The snatch from the rope is sufficient to make you lose your position and this problem will be a limiting factor in the next cut.

From the apex of the turn it is important to have a strong position in preparation for the pull. If your position during the pre-turn is correct, that is back straight and hips for-ward, then your position at the end of the turn should be good enough for the pull. Altering position during the turn so that you finish in a strong position is not recommended and you should try out the different positions and weight distributions during the pre-turn. As an intermediate step to compensate for a poor position during the turn, wait until the boat starts to pull again before pushing your hips forward.

## Key Points to Remember

1. Avoid changing position during the turn.
2. Keep your back straight and hips for-ward.

| Fault | Cause |
|-------|-------|
| 1. Turning too slow | a) Too much weight on the rear foot |
| 2. Turning too fast | a) Too much weight on the front foot |
|  | b) Breaking forward at the waist |

Fig 48   Keep your upper body strong throughout the turn.

# REACHING (LETTING GO OF THE ROPE)

The more you lean into the turn the more you need to let the rope out towards the boat. From the edge-change to the apex of the turn the skier is always leaning towards the boat, so it is only natural to let the arms extend in that direction. Holding on to the rope with both hands is impossible after a certain amount of lean without losing position. To overcome this problem and to assist with the deceleration you will need to learn the reaching technique.

The object of reaching is to let go of the rope with the hand furthest away from the boat just after the edge-change, pushing the controlling arm straight towards the boat so that full extension is reached before the apex of the turn. After the apex of the turn the ski will be turning back towards the wake and the arms will naturally come back towards the body. The free hand should be back on the handle before the boat starts to pull again.

## Dangers

Letting go of the rope may present some new problems because it will affect your weight distribution and therefore the way the ski turns. Also, reaching gives you the feeling of being in an exposed position as your body has less protection with your arms out of the way. Always wear a life-jacket when mono skiing as falling on to your side when in full reach may be painful without one.

*Fig 49   Reach with a straight arm directly towards the boat. The free arm should be kept under control.*

## Perfecting the Technique

To practise and perfect this technique, build up slowly as before to gain confidence.

As you change edges and the rope starts to move away from your body, let go with the outside hand, keeping it close to the handle. The controlling arm should not reach full extension yet. Concentrate on keeping the free hand close to the handle – this assists with control and will not feel too different from holding on to the rope with both hands. Just before the apex of the turn put the free hand back on the rope.

Once you are used to letting go of the rope and can do so without affecting your position, you are ready to extend your arm gradually until full extension is reached. Remember, the controlling arm should be extended directly towards the boat at all times and the free hand should not be allowed to fly out to the side. At the apex of the turn the ski starts to come around and the arms will come back towards the body. To assist with this and to gain a better position, the arms need to be lowered. A common mistake is to pull the arms in by bending them and then straighten them again as soon as the boat starts to pull. This problem occurs at the limit of your technique and you should look to your pre-turn for the solution. It is due to slack rope and may be cured by improving your deceleration.

## Weight

Reaching towards the boat may have the effect of changing your weight distribution and therefore altering the way in which the ski turns. By reaching towards the boat your

*Fig 50   Reach straight to the boat and keep your head up.*

arm will be further back than it would be if you were holding on with both hands and this means that you have more weight on the back foot than normal. The ski will turn more slowly than expected and the rate of turn may not be sufficient for the lean, thus causing a fall to the side. When reaching directly to the boat you need to keep your weight over the ski and push forward with hips and knees to compensate for reaching back. However, bending forward at the waist to bring the weight forward must be avoided.

## A Word of Warning

Be careful when reaching as the position of your arm controls the whole of your upper body. Throwing the arm out haphazardly will make your skiing inconsistent. Reaching forward leads to breaking forwards at the waist and a fast turn. Dropping the arm causes the shoulders to drop and may result in a sideways fall. Be positive and place the arm exactly where you want it to go.

## Key Points to Remember

1.   Keep your arm straight and pointing directly towards the boat at all times.
2.   Avoid pulling your arms in by bending them.
3.   Do not throw your free hand out to the side.

Fig 51  Reaching down and forwards will make you break at the waist.

Fig 52  Pulling the rope in with your arms may take away some slack.

Fig 53   Note how the arms are straight during the pull.

## CHAPTER SUMMARY

Having learned the basic techniques of pulling, decelerating, turning and reaching it is worth considering them together as you will find that they are interrelated. Although it is useful to practise each technique individually, it is necessary to understand how they affect each other and to know which area takes priority when dealing with problems.

The most difficult technique to master is that of slowing down during the pre-turn. This unfortunately determines both the quality of the turn and the ability to pull after it. A poor pre-turn means that you are going too fast into the turn and that most of the deceleration has to be made at the end of the turn. Failure to slow down will result in slack rope.

To compensate for a poor pre-turn, a rapid deceleration at the end of the turn is required. A sharp or 'hook' turn is the only way to slow down the ski in this situation, but be prepared for a strong pull from the boat. The remedy will only be effective if a good position has been maintained throughout, and more often than not you will find that the pull is too much for you to do anything. The usual result is therefore that you lose position and are pulled off your edge or over the front of your ski.

Slack rope and hook turns are the result of poor pre-turn technique and always show up at the limit of your ability. Priority should always be given to problems occurring in the pre-turn stage as they affect your skiing the most.

Reaching is an integral part of the pre-turn which means that a poor reach affects your ability to slow down. Also, careless reaching changes the position of your upper body and hence affects the turn.

Pulling, however, is a relatively easy technique to master and as such should be exploited to the full. A strong pull from the end of the turn to about a metre or two after the second wake, carried out while you are in position, will give you the required speed and leave you with plenty of room to slow down.

# 6 The Slalom Course

This chapter refines the techniques discussed in the previous chapter and is intended for those interested in slalom skiing. However, the chapter is also of relevance to those skiers who do not have access to a slalom course, especially the section on rough water skiing.

## Basics

The slalom course consists of six buoys, an entry gate and an exit gate. The boat passes through the entry gate and drives in a straight line at a constant speed through the centre of the course and out of the exit gates. The skier passes through the entry gate and then attempts to pass on the outside of the six buoys, completing the exercise by skiing through the exit gates. If all six buoys are rounded successfully and the skier has passed through both sets of gates, then the speed is increased. The speed is increased by 3 kph (2mph) increments after each suc-

cessful pass until a speed of 58 kph (36mph) is reached. On completion of a successful pass at this speed the rope is shortened, and this continues progressively until the skier falls.

Key

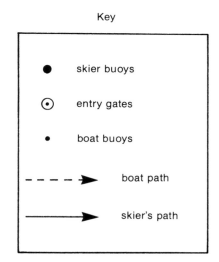

| | |
|---|---|
| ● | skier buoys |
| ⊙ | entry gates |
| • | boat buoys |
| - - - ▶ | boat path |
| —▶ | skier's path |

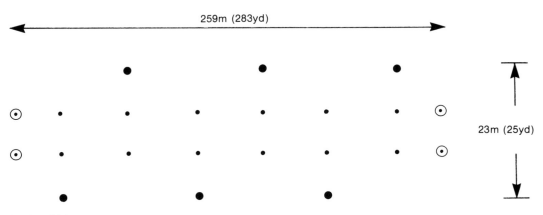

259m (283yd)

23m (25yd)

*Fig 54   Slalom course.*

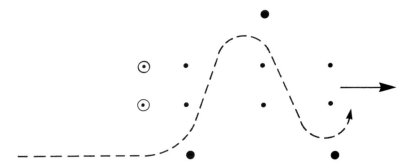

*Fig 55   Starting the turn before reaching the buoy will help establish rhythm.*

The slalom requires all the skills mentioned in the previous chapter and tests the skier to the full.

## FIRST ATTEMPTS

## Timing and Rhythm

Running the slalom course successfully requires timing and rhythm. Before attempting to go for the buoys, you need to establish whether it is possible to make six consecutive turns within the length of the slalom course. To do this the boat is driven down the centre of the course while you pull out to its right, ignoring the entry gates for the moment. Pull out to the width of the skier buoys and start cutting towards the second buoy approximately 10m (11yd) before arriving at the first. You should look for this second buoy after crossing the wake. As soon as you see it, turn, cross the wake and look for the third and so on until you reach the sixth buoy. At the sixth buoy, pull harder and ski around it, returning to the wake to pass through the exit gates.

The reason for taking this approach on the first attempts is that trying to ski around the buoys can disrupt any technique that you may have. Keeping the buoys some distance

in front of you ensures that you will at least see all six even if you make some mistakes and that you will have completed the six consecutive turns within the length of the slalom course. Skiing around the sixth buoy will give you an idea of the pull required.

Having established a rhythm the next step is to do the same as before, but this time skiing around the fifth and sixth buoys. Once this becomes easy take the fourth, fifth and sixth buoys and so on, repeating the procedure until it is possible to take all six buoys. It is important to follow this procedure because going for the course directly by taking the entry gate and going around the first buoy usually means that only one or two buoys are completed before you fall or lose sight of the buoys. It would also mean a loss of rhythm and confidence.

## IMPROVING TURNS

Slalom skiing uses all of the skills mentioned in the previous chapter but also requires exact timing since the correct place to turn is predetermined by the position of the buoys. Leaving aside the entry gates for the moment, we will concentrate on the approach to the buoy.

Turning close to the first buoy, pull as hard

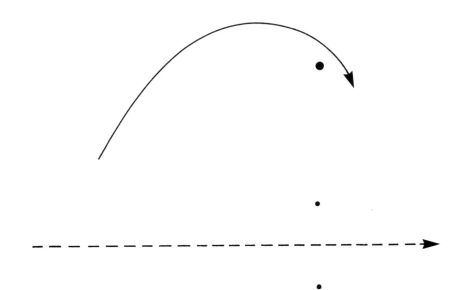

*Fig 56   Most of the turn is completed before the buoy.*

as possible through the wakes and start to change edges approximately 2m (2yd) after the second wake to initiate the turn. The object is to arrive at the buoy as early as possible, skiing wide of the line of skier buoys and reaching the apex of the turn just before the buoy. This means that the ski will already be turning back towards the wake by the time you pass the buoy.

The idea of pulling until only a few metres after the wake and starting the turn long before reaching the buoy may be difficult to grasp at first. Usually this technique results in turning inside the buoy on the first attempts. Increasing the length of the pull to 3-4m (3-4yd) after the wake may seem the logical answer to allow you to gain sufficient width at the turn, but this only causes you to ski straight to the buoy. Skiing straight to the buoy must be avoided as it reduces the opportunity of turning close to the buoy and also is less efficient in slowing the ski down. The usual result is that you turn late, usually

3-4m (3-4yd) past the buoy, making it difficult for you to reach the next buoy in time to ski wide and turn close to the buoy again. The effect may be cumulative so if you find you are getting to the buoys late, look back a few buoys to see if the turn was as good as it should have been. The answer to skiing inside the buoys is to pull harder rather than longer so that you have adequate speed to obtain the width but still have plenty of room to slow down.

## THE ENTRY GATE

A good start to the course is vital to give yourself the best opportunity of completing a successful pass. The reason for leaving this stage until last is that a poor entry will affect the whole of the pass.

# The Slalom Course

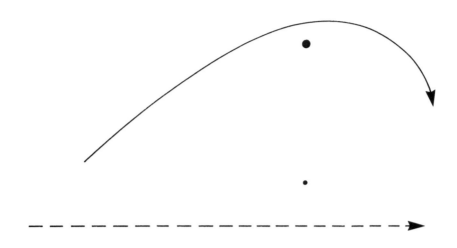

Fig 57   Skiing straight to the buoy means that you will turn late.

| Fault | Cause |
|---|---|
| 1.   Breaking forward at the waist | a)   Reaching forward during the pre-turn. This may be remedied by reaching straight to the boat and making sure your back is straight.<br>b)   Turning too fast. In turn, usually the result of a poor approach. Skiing too straight to the buoy means a rushed turn.<br>c)   Keeping the legs stiff through the wake |
| 2.   Slack rope | a)   Insufficient deceleration. To remedy, check that the edge-change is continuous and fast enough, and also check the lean and reach. |
| 3.   Tail of ski flipping out | a)   Stiff legs during the turn<br>b)   Turning too fast with too much weight on the front foot |
| 4.   Insufficient angle at end of turn | a)   Not enough lean during pre-turn |
| 5.   Skiing straight to the buoy | a)   Flat ski<br>b)   Looking down at the buoy<br>c)   Insufficient lean |
| 6.   Arriving late at the buoy | a)   Pulling too long<br>b)   Insufficient angle |

## The Cut

Pull out to the left of the boat on the approach to the course to about the width of the line of skier buoys, leaving sufficient time to adjust your position before starting the cut. The cut must be hard in order to reach the first buoy as early as possible. Timing the start of the cut so that you pass through the entry gates will come with experience, but for the moment you need only cross the wake somewhere in the vicinity of the entry gates. The main point is that the cut is hard and continuous. By cutting hard and gaining speed it is possible to be early on the first buoy, but be careful not to ski straight to the buoy or you will not slow down sufficiently to make a controlled turn.

# SHORT LINE SKIING

On completing a successful pass at the maximum speed for your age/sex category the rope will be shortened. Skiing on short line is an exhilarating new experience, but it should be remembered that the same basic principles apply.

A full length slalom line is 18.25m (19.95yd) long and has shortening loops to give lengths of 16, 14.25, 13 and 12m (17, 15.5, 14 and 13yd). There may be others, but they are not likely to be used. The correct way to secure the rope to a pylon or cleat is to hold the rope towards the skier's end and push it through the loop which will then tighten on itself when put over the pylon. If you push the wrong end of the rope through the loop then it will come undone when the rope is pulled. Check that the rope is attached securely as the pulls on short line skiing are greater than those on an 18.25m (19.95yd) rope.

The main difference when skiing on short line is that the force acting on the skier is

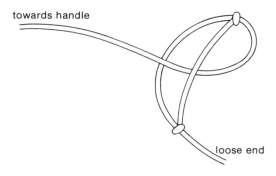

towards handle

loose end

Fig 58   A slalom shortening.

much greater. It may feel as if you are going a lot faster, but your average speed is really the same as before since you are covering the same distance in the same time. The impression of extra speed comes from the increased pull from the boat at the end of the turn. As the rope is shorter than before, the angle through which the rope must go for the skier to obtain the required width is greater.

This means that the direction of the pull has changed, so that as the skier reaches the end of the turn the pull is nearer to the direction in which he or she wishes to go. This means that the skier experiences a greater pull and hence accelerates more. The shorter the rope the greater the force and the greater the difficulty in maintaining position. The other problem caused by the increased acceleration is that of slowing down. Leaning more and ensuring that the reach is exploited to the full are more critical. Note that as the direction of the pull changes the direction of the reach will change accordingly. The shorter the rope the further back the reach will be at the apex of the turn.

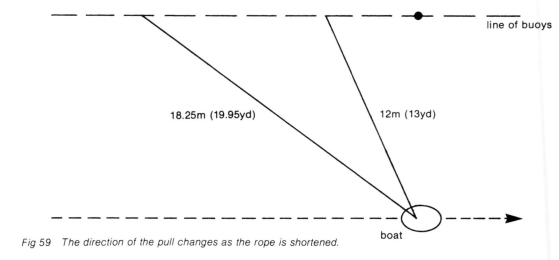

18.25m (19.95yd)     12m (13yd)

line of buoys

boat

Fig 59   The direction of the pull changes as the rope is shortened.

# ROUGH WATER SKIING

Skiing in ideal conditions is a rarity and more often than not you have to adapt the technique to the conditions. The two variables over which you have no control are wind and waves. Waves will cause the ski to jump out of the water, especially during the pre-turn, and the only way to reduce this effect is to flex the knees and keep a strong upper body. The wind introduces a variety of other problems and solutions.

## Tail Wind

If the wind is directly behind then it will have the effect of pushing the skier and assisting with acceleration, but making it difficult to slow down. Slowing down is further complicated by the waves that accompany the wind. Pulling out for the gates should be slightly earlier in windy conditions, thus allowing more time to slow down. How much earlier depends on the strength of the wind.

  The pull must be hard in order to gain sufficient angle, but it should be shorter than before to allow more time to slow down. Sufficient speed will have been gained with the assisting tail wind so a good edge-

change and lean are still required to slow the ski down. Pulling shorter and skiing straight to the buoy is guaranteed to result in too much speed during the turn. Speed in the turn, slack rope, a flat ski and waves combine to create a recipe for disaster.

## Head Wind

Skiing into a head wind is physically more demanding but allows for more mistakes. The overall effect is to slow the skier down, making it hard to accelerate but easier to slow down. A harder and longer pull is needed to build up the desired speed, but less work is required to slow down the ski. This means that less lean is required in the pre-turn, but be careful not to ski too narrow.

## Side Wind

A side wind is more complicated. If the wind is from left to right then it will assist the cut from left to right but resist the cut from right to left. Therefore short pulls from left to right, aimed at slowing you down, followed by longer, hard pulls from right to left are required. It is difficult to get a rhythm going and there is also the problem of slowing down on the rough side of the course with waves at an awkward angle.

The waves that accompany the wind affect the skier most during the pre-turn. Leaning towards the boat combined with the reduction in the pull produces a feeling of insecurity – especially when the skier is being buffeted by the waves. Going on to a flat ski only accentuates the effect of the waves and the ski will tend to jump both because of the speed and the flat surface of the ski. Changing edges quickly and bending the knees reduces the reliance on the lean and slows the ski down.

# 7 Trick Skiing

Trick skiing is the most accessible form of the sport as all you need is a boat and a pair of trick skis. Essentially, trick skiing is about performing rotations in various attitudes using one or two skis. Each trick is evaluated according to the degree of difficulty, and competitions are judged on the points accumulated during two twenty-second passes. Tricks peformed incorrectly are scored zero, and a fall before the twenty seconds have elapsed means that the remainder of the pass is forfeited. When putting a programme of tricks together a balance must be struck between doing difficult tricks with a high risk of falling, and settling for less but using all the time available. Although less physically demanding than mono skiing, trick skiing requires more self-discipline and patience. Restraining your enthusiasm to try the next trick before consolidating the one that you have just learned could be your biggest problem. However, tricks are fun and rapid progress can be sustained by following the basic rules. The key tricks are explained below and a good grounding in these is essential before progressing to more complex tricks.

The shorthand notation used to describe each trick is generally as follows:

1. Type of trick
   Wake trick                      W
   Line or step-over               L
   Toe hold                        T
2. Number of rotations
   360°                            3
   540°                            5
   720°                            7

3. Position at end of trick
   Backwards                       B
   Forwards                        F

With this system of shorthand it is possible to identify almost all tricks. Notice that if the trick is a 180° turn then there is no need to write the number of rotations. For example, a wake 180° turn starting forwards and finishing backwards is written WB. Similarly, a complicated trick like a wake step 540° front-to-back (i.e. turning one and a half rotations whilst stepping over the rope and landing backwards) is written WL5B.

## EQUIPMENT

The various types of ski are described in more detail in Chapter 11. A life-jacket is not absolutely necessary when trick skiing as the speeds involved are relatively slow. However, skiing without some form of buoyancy is dangerous and ill-advised. A high-buoyancy wet suit is recommended as it offers some degree of protection and is not as restrictive as a life-jacket.

## POSITION CHECK-LIST (TWO SKIS)

The position in which you start a trick will affect the performance of that trick, so it is essential that the correct position is assumed before every attempt.

*Fig 60   Before starting any trick, run through the position check-list.*

*Fig 61  The back is kept straight and the arms close to the body.*

Starting from the skis and working up:

1. Skis shoulder-width apart.
2. Weight on balls of feet.
3. Knees bent and flexible.
4. Back straight.
5. Head up and looking straight ahead.
6. Arms down and in with both hands on top.

The check-list above should be run through before every attempt to ensure that you are in the correct position. A lack of self-discipline at this point will increase the number of unnecessary falls.

## GETTING USED TO THE SKIS

When taking to the water for the first time the skis will feel very different to anything you have skied on before. The best way to get used to the skis is to spend plenty of time crossing the wake and learning how to control them.

In order to cross the wake the edges of the skis must be used to give the required grip on the water. The knees and ankles are used to put the skis on edge, but the upper body remains upright. Leaning with the body as you would on a normal pair of skis will only result in falling over sideways. Once you feel you have sufficient control over the skis try jumping the wake, remembering to maintain the correct position and bend your knees on landing. Excessive movements of the upper body lead to loss of control. One further exercise worth trying is to practise pulling your arms in without moving your upper body.

## CHOICE OF ROPE LENGTH AND BOAT SPEED

The optimum rope length depends on boat speed, which in turn depends upon the skier's weight and the surface area of the skis. If the speed is too slow the skis will ride low in the water, increasing the drag but adding to stability. The extra drag makes turning harder and is very tiring. If the speed is too fast the skis lose stability. As a general guideline, choose a speed that is slightly faster than that at which you feel comfortable. Once a suitable speed has been chosen the rope length may be altered. The ideal length is that which puts the skier in a position where the wake is between 2.5-3m (2.75-3yd) wide. This usually corresponds to a rope length of about 14-16m (15-17.5yd). If this length of rope puts you in a particularly turbulent part of the wake then extend the rope until you are in smoother water.

The following tricks are explained for those skiers who prefer to turn to the right or are right-footed.

### Two-Ski Sideslide (*SS*)

The object is to turn the skis sideways and return to the front after a short pause. Both hands are kept on the handle at all times. Ski directly behind the boat and run through the position check-list.

To initiate the turn, pull the rope gently, moving the handle to the left and turning your hips to the right. The skis will start to turn to the right but you should keep your head and shoulders facing the boat. If the skis feel difficult to turn and you start skiing towards the wake then you have too much weight on your heels. Once the skis are sideways they will break free of the water and start to slide. If your weight is not directly over the skis they

Fig 62 *Twisting the arm and turning the hips gives the rotation.*

Fig 63 *Notice how the arms are close to the body.*

will slip towards the boat. Another problem will occur if you allow the handle to be pulled away from your body during the turn, since in this case the leading edge is likely to catch in the water and stop abruptly.

Once you feel more confident, extend the amount of time you spend sideways.

## 180° Turn (*B, F*)

The object is to turn to the backwards position and then return to the front the way you came. Check your position before you begin.

To initiate the turn, pull the rope in slowly and firmly, moving the rope to the left. Let go of the rope with the right hand and twist the handle in a clockwise direction with your left hand. The free hand should be reaching around the back to meet the handle with the whole of the body turning simultaneously. Movement of the upper body – the result of turning with your shoulders first and leaving the rest of your body to follow – will cause you to turn off-axis.

Before returning to the front, straighten your back and keep your head up. Let go of the rope with the right hand and turn to the front the way you came, keeping the rope close to your body.

## 360° Turn (*3F*)

The object is to turn to the back, pause, and continue to the front turning in the same direction. The duration of the pause is reduced until the turn is continuous.

The turn is initiated in the same way as the 180° turn, but the emphasis is put on reaching around the back with the free hand to take the handle. This trick should be thought of as two 180° turns until the hesitation in the backwards position is negligible.

The sideslide 180° and 360° turns are called the basics and should be perfected along with their associated reverses before progressing further. Persevering with these tricks until they can be performed consistently well pays dividends in the long run.

| Fault | Cause |
|-------|-------|
| 1. Falling towards the boat | a) Jerking the rope and so transferring the weight on to the heels during the turn |
| | b) Letting your arms out |
| 2. Falling away from the boat | a) Too much weight on your heels at the start |
| | b) Pulling with your body |
| 3. Edge of skis catching water | a) Letting your arms out during the initial part of a front-to-back turn |
| | b) Opening your skis whilst turning to the front |

# WAKE TRICKS

The next step is to try 180° and 360° turns in the air using the wake as a ramp. To start with the tricks are learned flat, that is the skis do not leave the water.

# 180° Wake (*WB, WF*)

There are four variations on the 180° turn and a choice of two wakes from which to do them. With so many choices, some are bound to be easier than others. The easiest of these is the front-to-back (*WB*), starting from outside and finishing in the centre of the wake. Right-footed skiers or skiers preferring to turn to the right should use the left wake.

Skiing outside the left wake, position yourself a metre away from the crest. Check your position then ski towards the wake, starting to pull on the rope so that your arms are in just as you arrive at the crest of the wake. Do not jump – think of the trick as a surface trick. Finish the trick directly behind the boat as this will make it easier to stabilise.

The next step is to try the same trick but starting behind the boat and doing it on the right wake. This means that you finish the trick skiing backwards outside the right wake. There are two problems you need to be aware of. Firstly, as you ski away from the centre of the wake the force of the rope increases and therefore requires a harder pull to get the arms in. Secondly, because you will be finishing the trick on the slope of the wake you need to concentrate on bending your knees on landing and turning on axis. After stabilising backwards outside the wake, check your position.

For the forward wake trick (*WF*) cut towards the wake, turning to the front the way you came. Judging the correct place to turn is difficult at first, but for the moment the most important thing is to keep your arms in during the turn. If you have difficulty in skiing backwards outside the wake, turn backwards behind the boat and practise crossing the wake whilst in this position.

# Hand-to-Hand 360° Wake (*W3F*)

This trick starts with you skiing in the forwards position outside the left wake. The main difficulties lie with rotation and passing the handle.

Standing about a metre outside the left wake, ski to the top of the wake, pulling the rope so that your arms are fully in just as you pass through the wake. Start the turn and quickly reach around your back for the rope. Do not let go of the rope until the other hand has a good grip on it. Approaching the front, reach quickly with the free hand to take the

Fig 64    Put the skis on edge by using your
          knees and ankles.

Fig 65    The turn is identical to the surface
          180° turn.

Fig 66    Bend your knees on landing.

Fig 67    Edge the skis and keep your arms in.

*Fig 68    Turn to the front, keeping the back
straight and arms in.*

*Fig 69    Bend your knees on landing. Do not
let your arms reach full extension.*

handle. Landing with two hands on the
handle increases your chances of success.
Good rotation is achieved by edging the skis
hard into the wake and keeping your back
straight and arms in.

## 360° Wake Helicopter (*W3F*)

This trick is the same as the previous trick
but does not require passing the handle. The
advantage is gained by using the rope to

| Fault | Cause |
|---|---|
| 1. Falling towards boat on landing | a) Insufficient pull<br>b) Stiff legs |
| 2. Falling away from boat | a) Pulling with your body<br>b) Putting too much weight on your heels at the start |
| 3. Falling sideways | a) Pulling with the body<br>b) Insufficient turn |
| 4. Catching edge | a) Letting your arms out<br>b) Turning too early |

assist with the rotation. If you prefer to turn to the right then your right hand needs to reach around your back to take the handle. The ideal way to do this is to pull the rope in hard, giving yourself enough slack to quickly reach around your back and take the rope. Once your right hand has the handle, let go with the left and quickly hold the rope in front to stop spinning out of the wrap prematurely. If you pulled sufficiently then you will have enough time to take hold of the rope before the slack takes up. Once you have the rope securely, rearrange your arm and the handle so that your arm rather than the rope is around your back and your palm is facing outwards and holding the handle at the bottom.

*Fig 70   Wrapped up for a wake 360° front-to-front.*

To get used to turning, try practising behind the boat. Again, check your position and, when ready, initiate the turn by gently pulling the rope to the side with your left hand. Turn slowly and maintain your position. Keep practising this until you feel comfortable. Only try it on the wake when it is possible to finish the trick in a good position.

A common problem at this point is letting the arms out during the turn. This will slow the turn and is unnecessary as there is no force acting on the arm until you reach the forwards position.

To try the trick on the wake, wrap up behind the boat and ski outside the left wake in the forwards position. Stand about a metre outside the wake and check your position. Cut towards the wake and as your skis pass through the wake, start the turn. Resist the temptation to throw your body, jump or turn too fast. Again, it should be thought of as only a surface trick. Major problems are letting your arms out and turning too early. Both result in slowing the turn and causing the edges of the skis to catch in the wake. The reverse should be learned as soon as possible after the basic.

## Generating Lift

Doing wake tricks in the air usually presents some problems as skiers try to jump in order to get the skis clear of the water. Only a few tricks actually need a physical jump and, as a rule, jumping should be avoided since it involves a change in position.

Lift is generated by using the wake as a ramp, and only requires the correct approach and good timing to obtain all the 'air time' you will need. Edging the skis all the way up the wake whilst maintaining position and timing the turn so that the skis just start to turn as you reach the crest are the important factors to be aware of.

## Key Points to Remember

1. Your legs must be strong as you ski up the wake to avoid crushing.
2. Skiing up the wake, performing the trick and landing should be done as a continuation of the cut. Cutting to the top of the wake, stopping and then doing the trick should be avoided.
3. Edge the skis all the way to the top of the wake.
4. Turn just as the skis are passing through the crest of the wake.

## ONE-SKI TRICKS

The positioning of the bindings on a single trick ski means that an asymmetrical position must be assumed. The rear foot has to be set at an angle to allow the legs maximum flexibility. Tricks on one ski require balance and good ski control and hence priority is given to flexing the legs. The drawback is that the ski is much easier to turn in one direction than the other. In fact the ski tends to crab instead of travelling in a straight line. This is normal and is a good sign as it means that you have a natural attitude on the ski.

## POSITION CHECK-LIST

1. Ankles bent.
2. Knees bent and pushed apart.
3. Back straight.
4. Both hands on top.

This unusual position takes some getting used to and you should practise crossing the wake until you have reasonable control over the ski. Remember to use the edge of the ski and keep a strong upper body position. A slightly faster boat speed may be required.

## Sideslide (*SS*)

The same principles apply as for the two-ski sideslide but an extra effort is required to turn the hips for the reverse because of the position of the feet. Having only one ski to stand on reduces the stability, so it is necessary to be aware of your weight distribution prior to and during the turn.

## 180° Turn (*B,F*)

Check your position. The turn is initiated in the same way as a two-ski 180° turn. Problems occur as a result of a loss of balance and incorrect pulling. There is more drag skiing on one ski so a stronger pull is needed. Most falls happen because of the difficulty of maintaining position and correct weight distribution whilst pulling.

## 360° Turn (*3F*)

In the same way as the two-ski 360° turn this trick should be thought of as two 180° turns. Difficulties with this and other one-ski basic tricks are essentially the same as those with the two-ski basics (*see* page 65).

## One-Ski Wake Tricks

Maintaining position and weight distribution whilst cutting to the wake and the additional problem of landing on one ski are the main areas of interest here. Obviously, landing backwards on one ski is difficult for the first few attempts, but exaggerating the knee bend on landing helps. If the problem of skiing backwards outside the wake persists then practise crossing the wake backwards. Bending at the waist, whilst helping to absorb some shock, ultimately leads to a loss of balance and must be avoided.

Fig 71   Wake 360°.

Fig 72  Remember that the wake 180° is
        similar to the 180° turn behind the boat.

Fig 73  Bending the knees on landing is
        critical on one ski.

This concludes the section on the basic surface and wake tricks on one and two skis. A good grounding in these tricks and their associated reverses is strongly recommended.

# INTERMEDIATE TRICKS

## Wrapped 180° One Ski (B,F)

The 180° wrap has the same points value as the normal 180° surface turn but is particularly useful as a positional trick. In other words it makes a good starting-point for more difficult tricks and also takes less time to perform.

The object is to turn to the backwards position whilst keeping two hands on the handle and looking at the boat. To get a feel for the trick turn right round, holding the rope with both hands and returning to the front immediately. Next, try to turn the ski and your

Fig 74  Finish the trick with hands close to
        the body.

71

Fig 75  *Keep the back straight.*

On turning backwards your arms will wrap around your body and should be waist high. They may, however, be pulled out by the boat, causing you to turn to the front. To avoid this, keep your left hand close to your side by bringing your right arm across your stomach and pressing it firmly against your body. Once you are able to stay facing backwards, experiment with your position and slowly stand more upright until you can keep your back straight and legs flexible.

The reverse should be tried but will be harder to hold in the backwards position as it is more difficult to turn the ski in that direction. It is not important to hold this position for the moment, but it will be useful to be able to do so when you come to try the 360° back-to-back.

## 360° Back-to-Back (*3B*)

This has the same points value as the 360° front-to-front but is easier and faster. Holding on to the rope with two hands at all times, turn into the 180° wrap and hold it. Check your position, then slowly turn to the front and instead of stopping, continue into the reverse 180° wrap. Don't try to hold the reverse wrap but return to the front immediately. If you are in a good position then continue into the basic 180° wrap to complete the reverse back-to-back.

## Key Points to Remember

1. Keep your back straight.
2. Turn slowly.
3. Keep your arms in when passing the front position.

hips around whilst looking at the boat, making sure your back is straight. The position may feel uncomfortable at first but will soon become familiar. Check that your legs are not stiffening up and keep your back straight. The true value of this trick becomes apparent when it is possible to remain in the backwards position whilst looking at the boat.

*Fig 76   Keep the arms close to the body during the turn.*

| Fault | Cause |
|---|---|
| 1. Falling towards the boat | a) Not leaning away from the boat whilst holding the basic wrap<br>b) Letting your arms out as you pass the forwards position |
| 2. Falling sideways | a) Not keeping your back straight |
| 3. Being unable to continue past the forwards position | a) Letting your arms out<br>b) Too much weight on your back foot |

## Wake 360° Back-to-Back (*W3B*)

This trick has the same points value as the W3F but is easier and faster. The W3B is a combination of the wrapped 180° (*F*) and the reverse (*WB*). In fact the upper body only turns through 180° whilst the ski turns through 360°.

Skiing directly behind the boat, turn into the wrapped 180° and hold the position. Straighten your back and put equal weight on both feet. Edging towards the left wake, without altering position turn at the top of the wake. The turn resembles the 180° (*WB*) and it helps to think of this trick as you perform the rotation. Remember to flex your legs on landing.

The reverse is slightly more difficult and you will need to concentrate on timing the turn at the top of the wake and keeping the arms in at the start. If the arms are extended when passing the forwards position the last part of the turn is impossible.

*Fig 77  The wake 180° turns are fast and easy when using two hands.*

| Fault | Cause |
|---|---|
| 1. Falling towards the boat | a) Arms too far away from your body<br>b) Too much weight on your back foot |
| 2. Falling away from the boat | a) Leaning away too much |
| 3. Falling sideways | a) Not edging the ski to the top of the wake<br>b) Incorrect start position |

## Two-ski Step-over (*LB, LF*)

Step-overs and their associated tricks involve one leg passing over the rope or line during the turn, and are sometimes called line tricks.

## Line Back (*LB*)

The difficulty with this trick is that you have to do several things at the same time. Pulling the rope in and down, lifting the ski and turning all have to be done in quick succession. You could practise pulling the rope in and down in preparation.

The turn is initiated by pulling the rope down and lifting the knee, turning the hips then pushing the knee over the rope. The ski should follow the knee over the rope. Falling away from the boat is caused by bending at the waist during the turn.

## Line Front (*LF*)

This is quite a difficult trick to learn and you may find it easier to approach by learning the line back (*LB*) first.

Skiing backwards on two skis, slowly lower the rope until it is just above the back of the knees. Let go of the handle with your left hand and reach between your legs to take the rope. Let go of the rope with your right hand and straighten your back, holding the left arm up as high as possible. The right hand needs to be held up and back to help keep your shoulders up during the turn.

Fig 78  Pull the rope in and down, turning your hips and pushing your knee over the rope.

Fig. 79  Notice how much the knee is bent.

Fig 80   Try not to drop the shoulders.

Fig 81   Put the ski down and straighten the back.

To turn, lift up the back of the left ski by bending your knee and turning your hips. As you start to turn, reach forward with your right hand to take the rope.

Falling away from the boat is the biggest problem as it is all too easy to bend at the waist or lean away whilst lifting the ski. Care must therefore be taken at the beginning of the turn not to lose position.

## INTRODUCTION TO TOE HOLDS (*TB, TF*)

Before attempting toe holds make sure that you have a quick-release device or a suitable toe strap. The driver should also be aware that you are trying toe holds so that, if the rope does not release, he knows to stop the boat instantly.

Put your foot firmly into the toe hold and regain your balance. The correct position is:

weight directly over the ski, back straight and arms out to the side for balance. Further, the leg you are standing on should be bent and the leg controlling the rope should be slightly in to give better control.

The turn is initiated by turning the leg and hips. If position is maintained then the turn

Fig 82   Start position.

Fig 83   Control is maintained by keeping the rope in.

*Fig 84   Keep a straight back at all times.*

will be on axis. Most problems stem from bending at the waist or letting the rope out. Letting the leg out and bending at the waist are related as it is difficult to keep a straight back if your leg is fully extended.

Once in a backwards position, stabilise by flexing your knee and keeping control with the leg holding the rope. Straighten your back and hold the rope half-way between full extension and being fully in. Before turning to the front, arch your back so that your weight is over the ski.

Turning to the front is again initiated by the movement of the leg and hips. As you turn to the front, reach forward with the hands to reduce the possibility of falling backwards. Again, keep in the leg with the rope.

## SUMMARY

The tricks outlined above are only a small selection of those possible, but they do provide a good basis for progressing to the more difficult tricks. Taking care to check your position before attempting any trick and following the basic guidelines will ensure rapid progress.

# 8  Jumping

Jumping is perhaps the most exhilarating of the three main events of water skiing but specialist equipment and good preparation are necessary to minimise the danger involved. A majority of falls in the early stages may be avoided by having a clear idea of what to expect and what to do. Before considering an attempt at the jump you should be able to ski competently on two skis.

## POSITION CHECK-LIST

1. Skis shoulder-width apart.
2. Weight on balls of feet.
3. Knees bent.
4. Back straight.
5. Arms in and down.
6. Head up.

### Basic Technique

The handle is held by the same grip used for slalom skiing, with the left hand on top. This position does not change at all during the approach, the jump or the landing, and it should be memorised. Before going over the jump, practise on the jump skis to become familiar with the skiing position. Jumping the wake will give additional confidence.

## BOAT DRIVING

The boat speed should be approximately 35–37 kph (22–23 mph) and the path parallel to the jump, passing close to the right-hand side.

## FIRST ATTEMPTS

The ramp is very slippery so it is important to have equal weight on both skis and weight on the balls of your feet. On the approach, pull out to the left of the boat, leaving plenty of time to prepare and get into position. To maintain your position outside the boat's wake you have to lean away from the boat. However, it is important to make sure that

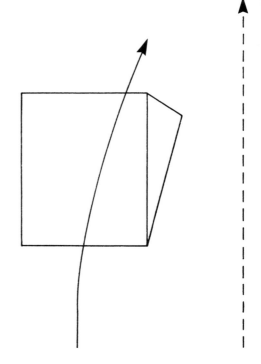

Fig 85   On the approach to the ramp, flatten the skis so that the path taken up the ramp is diagonal.

you are not leaning away from the boat as you go over the ramp otherwise the skis will slide out from underneath you.

Approaching the ramp, get into position. Looking straight ahead, aim for the middle of the ramp. A metre or two before reaching it, flatten the skis by putting equal weight on both feet and allow the boat to pull you directly towards it. By flattening the skis you are allowing the boat to pull you back towards the wake and hence the path taken up the ramp is diagonal from left to right.

The ramp, if properly lubricated, is faster than the water and feels very slippery, showing up clearly any incorrect weight distribution. The direction in which you fall will also indicate to you where you put too much weight. Thus falling away from the boat suggests that you were leaning away, while falling backwards suggests that your weight was on your heels. Remember that the weight must be directly over the skis for you to land on your feet.

Remember too that the position remains the same both on the ramp and in the air. Holding the arms down and looking straight ahead will ensure that good position is maintained. On landing, look straight ahead and try to keep a strong position.

## Key Points to Remember

1. Maintain position at all times.
2. Have equal weight on both feet just before the ramp.
3. Weight on balls of feet.
4. Look straight ahead.
5. Keep arms in and down.

*Fig 86 Lean too far back and you will fall backwards.*

Fig 87   Leaning away from the boat will have this effect.

Figs 88-90   The position remains the same at all times.

Fig 89

Fig 90

# Jumping

| Fault | | Cause | |
|-------|---|-------|---|
| 1. Collapsing on the ramp | | a) | Not keeping the legs strong |
| 2. Falling backwards on the ramp | | a) | Putting your weight on your heels |
| | | b) | Collapsing on the ramp |
| 3. Falling away from the boat | | a) | Continuing to lean away on reaching the ramp |
| 4. Falling forwards on landing | | a) | Looking down |
| | | b) | Stiff legs |
| 5. Falling backwards in the air | | a) | Straight body, usually caused by lifting the arms up |

After a few successful attempts the boat should accelerate gradually to around 43kph (27 mph) and the boat path should be moved further out. The final boat path will be approximately 10m (11yd) from the ramp and parallel to it. If a skier is having difficulties, reduce the distance from the ramp.

Before continuing, it is important to consolidate your jumping technique. Gaining confidence now will prevent falls later. It is not necessary that you land cleanly on your feet, but it is a bonus if you are able to do this as it is a sign of good technique.

## SINGLE WAKE CUT

The object is to time the pull out to the ramp so that you are still moving away from the wake as you make the jump. By moving away from the wake you will be going slightly faster than the boat and it is this extra speed that is the key to longer jumps. The stronger pull from the boat makes the landings easier but requires good timing and position.

The two problems that have to be faced are staying in position and keeping the correct weight distribution during the cut, but these will take care of themselves if you are aware of them and attempt to build up the cut slowly and carefully.

Skiing just to the left of the boat's wake, get into position. Leaving plenty of time, aim for the centre of the ramp. The important thing is to continue cutting until a few metres in front of the ramp without going on to flat skis. By doing this you are building and maintaining speed all the time. Only when you are on flat skis are you slowing down.

Ensure that, as you start the cut, your weight is directly over the skis. It is natural to put more weight on the heels when cutting so it is important to be aware of this problem and push your knees forward to keep your weight over the skis. During the cut you will also be leaning away, so it will be necessary to flatten the skis prior to reaching the ramp to obtain equal weight on the skis.

Gradually leave the cut, remembering that the later your cut, the harder you have to pull in order to reach the ramp in time. Pulling harder may affect your position, and adjustments to your position at the start of the cut may be needed. Altering position during the cut is not recommended.

### Refusing

By cutting later, you are bound to have the occasional cut which feels wrong. Rather

Fig 91   Leaning too far back on the cut will lead to problems in the air.

# *Jumping*

Fig 92  *Landing on your feet is a bonus, but sitting back will reduce the strain on your knees and back.*

than going over the ramp it may be better to refuse. Refusing means letting go of the rope just before the ramp and skiing past the ramp on the left-hand side. Never try to cut back towards the boat's wake to avoid the ramp as you will get slack rope and lose control. Sometimes it may be a good idea to practise refusing so that you know what to do in case of difficulty.

## Key Points to Remember

1. Always aim for the centre of the ramp. Aiming for the bottom right corner means that there is not much room for error.
2. Keep your skis on edge from the beginning of the cut to 1–2m (1–2yd) in front of the ramp.
3. The position and weight distribution must not be affected by the cut.

| Fault | Cause |
|---|---|
| 1. Falling sideways towards the boat | a) Arriving at the ramp too early and cutting back towards the boat<br>b) Arms pulled out on the cut |
| 2. Falling backwards | a) Putting your weight on your heels during the cut |
| 3. Falling forwards | a) Breaking forward at the waist on the ramp<br>b) Looking down |

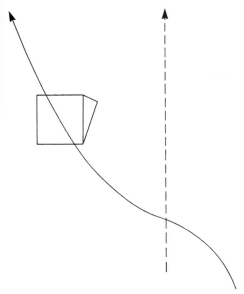

Fig 93   The three-quarter cut.

# THE THREE-QUARTER CUT

The three-quarter cut is the next stage and involves cutting from outside the right-hand wake. Again leaving plenty of time, position yourself so that you are 10–15m (11–16yd) outside the right wake. Check your position and make any adjustments before you start the cut. The object is to cut continuously from the end of the turn to a few metres in front of the ramp. The turn must be slow in order to maintain position and the angle through which the skis turn should be such as to point them towards the centre of the ramp. Keeping the skis pointing to the centre at all times during the cut means that the pull required to sustain this line of attack is easy

Fig 94   Pulling too hard at the beginning of the cut means that you will have to flatten off too early.

at the beginning, becoming gradually harder as you approach the ramp. This technique ensures that you are pulling hard through the wakes and hardest just before the ramp, and means that your skis are continually on edge.

## Key Points to Remember

1.   Turn slowly.
2.   Cut continuously.
3.   Maintain position.
4.   Keep shoulders turned away from ramp.

| Fault | Cause |
|---|---|
| 1.   Flattening skis too early | a)   Turning too fast |
| | b)   Pulling too hard at the beginning of the cut |
| 2.   Arms being pulled out after crossing the wake | a)   Shoulders turning to the boat |

Fig 95   *Cut all the way to the ramp, keeping your arms in and your head and shoulders turned away from the ramp.*

## ADVANCED JUMPING TECHNIQUE

Once you have consolidated your jumping technique and are safely cutting all the way to the ramp on a three-quarter cut, it is time to progress on to the counter-cut. The idea is to get as wide of the boat as possible on the approach to the ramp so that the pull of the boat may be used to generate maximum speed.

To get wide of the boat on the approach it is necessary to make a counter-cut, that is a cut across the wake from left to right building up sufficient speed and momentum to obtain greater width prior to the cut towards the ramp.

Assuming the correct body position, that is arms in, knees bent and skis shoulder-width apart, pull out to the left of the boat by edging the right ski and lifting the left. As you get to within about 45° of the boat, pull your arms across your body and flatten your skis. Just before you start to drift back, turn the skis through 90° and push hard on the left-hand ski, concentrating on keeping your shoulders turned away from the boat, keeping the skis on edge and pulling as hard as possible through the wakes. After the second wake, lift the right ski and continue to push hard on the left ski. Again, as you get to within 45° of the

Fig 96  Lift the ski after the wake to get extra speed on the counter-cut.

Fig 97  Knowing when to refuse is a valuable asset.

boat, pull your arms across your body and flatten your skis. It is the speed generated on the counter-cut, combined with the timing of the moment at which you pull the rope across your body and flatten the skis, that will send you wide of the boat.

Judging the correct place to start your counter-cut is critical if you are to be in the right place to start your cut to the ramp. Make use of the 150 and 180m (164 and 197yd) buoys at the beginning of the jump course rather than using other markers to judge your cut. Also take into consideration the wind conditions as they will make a great difference to the timing of the counter-cut.

Skiing wide of the boat means that it is easier to cut later yet arrive at the ramp earlier than would otherwise have been the case. Avoid the temptation to turn too fast as it will affect your position and you may reach the ramp too early. Make sure that you use the period when skiing on flat skis to make any adjustments to your position before making the turn. The turn should be well measured so that the initial pull is smooth and it is easy to maintain position. Cut all the way to the ramp, keeping the skis on edge all the way.

# 9 Barefoot

Any good mono skier can learn to barefoot providing that the boat is powerful enough. A boat which is capable of maintaining a speed of 58kph (36mph) and keeping a flat stretch of water clear of debris are the main requirements. There are several methods of starting, three of which are outlined below.

## Step Off One Ski

Using a slalom ski with a loose-fitting binding, stand in the flat water just outside the wake. Right-footed skiers should stand outside the right wake. To make the set-up easier keep the boat speed at approximately 49kph (30mph) until you are in position.

A boat speed in the region of 55-60kph (34-37mph) should be sufficient for most skiers. Holding the handle with both hands on top, keep your back straight and look straight ahead. Slowly place your free foot in the water in front of the skiing foot, increasing the weight on the foot by bending the skiing leg. By keeping the rope low the position will be stable. Once a majority of the weight is supported by the free foot, quickly drop the ski and place the foot forward so that it is level with the other foot. The drag increases once the ski is off so it is important to keep the arms low in order to remain in a strong position.

## Deep Water Start

It is important to have a good wet suit with tight-fitting legs and built-in buoyancy. However, wearing a life-jacket underneath the wet suit will give the required protection whilst presenting less resistance to the water.

Once in the water, hold the handle with both hands and keep your arms straight. Lie on your back and cross your toes over the rope. Until you are ready, keep your head out of the water so that you can see what you are doing. When the rope is taut, put your head into the water and arch your back. The driver will take this as the signal to start. As the boat starts to pull, maintain position. If you are having any difficulties at this stage remember to uncross your feet before letting go of the handle. As you emerge from the water, slowly sit up and pull your arms in and down so that you are skiing on your bottom. Maintain this position with your feet still crossed over the rope until sufficient speed has been built up. When ready, uncross your feet, bend your legs and place your feet in the water. This method of starting is uncomplicated but requires some strength to hold position, especially at the very start.

## Starting from a Knee Board or Disc

Perhaps the easiest and safest way to get started on barefoot. Sit on top of the board at a speed of approximately 20-25kph (12-16mph) with both feet forward and hanging over the front edge. By moving your weight backwards or forwards it should be possible to ride smoothly without bouncing. Once stable, bend your knees and put your heels into the water gently and slowly. At this point the boat will steadily accelerate up to barefooting speed. Don't be too anxious to

Fig 98   Barefooting on one leg.

*Fig 99  The deep water start.*

stand up but wait for the boat to pick up speed. At the right moment slowly increase the pressure on your feet. Once a majority of your weight is supported by your feet the board will slide out from underneath your bottom.

## SUMMARY

If, during any of the above starts, severe spray is encountered when placing your feet into the water, try pointing your toes slighly inwards or increasing the boat's speed. Falling forwards is a fault generally caused by straight legs or letting the rope go too high.

# 10 Competitive Water Skiing

One of the attractions of water skiing is that it offers plenty of opportunities to ski against people of a similar standard. The main aims of competition are to win or make a personal best performance. In order to do either of these a knowledge of the important rules and various tactics of competition skiing is required to maximise your chances of success. Water skiing competitions are usually based on a 'sudden death' approach so that one mistake early on may mean the end of your tournament. However, this applies to all skiers no matter how good their previous performances, and it is often the case that well-prepared skiers are able to beat those skiers with higher scores on paper. Good preparation and appraisal of the prevailing conditions are essential.

The three events of competitive water skiing are slalom, tricks and jump. If a competition features all three events, then there is usually an overall prize calculated from the points accumulated from each event.

## SLALOM

Looking at the site and water conditions, decide the maximum speed at which you would normally expect to make a successful pass. In deciding on a suitable starting speed, choose one which will give you three to four successful passes before reaching the pass which you expect to give the most problems. Three to four passes is sufficient to 'warm up' whilst leaving enough energy for

the last pass. Consideration should also be given to the direction of the prevailing wind, remembering that it is usually easier to complete a pass skiing into the wind. Therefore, make your decision with due regard to the direction of the wind on your last expected pass. If you expect only one or two buoys at this pass then it doesn't matter if the wind is behind. However, if you are experiencing more the decision is more difficult.

If you are the first skier to start then there is no choice except to ski as planned. If you are starting down the list then use the opportunity to watch other skiers and make an objective assessment of their performances to gain a better idea of the conditions. Don't just look at the results of other skiers, especially if they are poor, but look for any underlying trend before downgrading your expectations.

If you are skiing near to the end of the list and your main rivals have already skied, you will have an idea of what is needed to win. If you require only one or two buoys at a particular speed then approach the course bearing this number in mind. There is no need to get a 'good' first buoy to make up time if only one or two buoys are needed. If you need three or more then you will have to take a chance and make sure that the first buoy is good.

Finally, a common mistake by many skiers is to ski much too cautiously on the earlier passes. This usually means that the skier will reach and lean less than normal and results in too much speed at the buoys and possibly

*Fig 100    Confidence and determination are the keys to success in competition.*

skiing narrow. The whole purpose of the first few passes is to compensate for any elementary errors such as stiff legs, and build up rhythm and confidence.

## Scoring

The number of buoys scored in slalom depends on where the skier falls or at which point in the course a buoy is missed. If a skier reaches the line of skier buoys whilst in a skiing position the score is a quarter of a buoy. If the skier makes a turn on the outside of the buoy and returns past the line of skier buoys the score is a half. A whole buoy is scored if the skier reaches the boat's wake before the next set of boat buoys. Note that if the entry gate is missed the whole pass scores zero.

If you elect to start at a higher speed than the minimum set for the competition and fail to make your first pass, then the score is the number of buoys made on that pass, but calculated at the start speed.

## Rerides

A reride is given when a skier has an unfair advantage or disadvantage over the other skiers. The main form of reride encountered in slalom skiing is due to incorrect boat speed, but it may also be given for unfair water conditions, obstructions etc. In the case of incorrect boat speed, a skier is deemed to have had an unfair advantage if the boat speed was too slow, or a disadvantage if the speed was too fast.

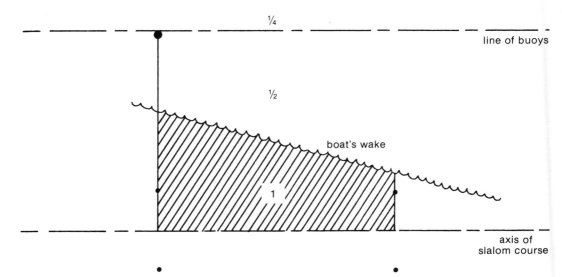

Fig 101   *Showing the scoring of points in slalom.*

If the speed is too slow then the skier is shown a red flag. The red flag signifies to the skier that the reride is compulsory. If the skier did not complete that particular pass then he or she may not improve the score on the reride. For example, if three buoys were scored on the first attempt when the speed was slow then it is not likely that the skier would have scored more if the speed had been correct. So on the reride the skier may only score a maximum of three buoys even if the pass is completed successfully. If the skier made all six buoys and is then given a reride for a slow speed he or she has the option of taking the pass again or proceeding to the next pass. If the second option is taken and the skier completes the pass then both passes score. If he fails to make the pass at the higher speed then the score will be that gained at the lower speed.

If the speed is too fast, a green flag is shown. This means that the reride is optional. If the skier did not complete the pass successfully then he or she is given the option of taking the pass again or settling for

the score already made. If the pass was completed then the green flag will be shown but no reride is given and the next pass has to be taken.

It is important to understand these considerations as it may be necessary to make a decision on the spur of the moment.

## TRICKS

The main objective of competitive trick skiing is to design two sequences of different tricks lasting approximately twenty seconds each in order to accumulate the maximum number of points. There are certain restrictions on the way that tricks are arranged, and repetitions of a trick will not be scored. The main restriction is that the reverse of a trick must be completed immediately after the basic if it is to score. The only exception to this is if it is necessary to do any type of 180° turn between the basic and reverse. The other restriction applies to the trick numbers, that is that only one basic and

Fig 102  Make sure that all the tricks count.

one reverse may be performed under each number.

A list of tricks and the order in which they are to be performed must be submitted to the judges prior to the event and only tricks which correspond to those on the list will be considered.

## Designing a Trick Programme

When planning a trick programme it is important not to get carried away and go for the most difficult and highest-scoring you can think of. There is no point in having a high-scoring run if the chances of doing it are slim. Your main concern should be to use all of the time available and arrange the tricks as best you can.

One way of designing a programme is to write down all the tricks that you are able to do in order of difficulty or consistency. By putting easy tricks at the top of the list and the more uncertain ones towards the end a sensible decision on which tricks to include and where to put them can be made. If you have more tricks than you are able to use then consider if it is worth while to do easy tricks quickly in preference to difficult ones slowly. A run full of fancy tricks is often worth no more points than one packed with easy tricks. Any tricks which are not quite perfected should ideally not be included in the run at all, but if you have no other choice make sure that they come at the very end. Tricks which require some preparation, such as the wrap, could be put at the very beginning of the run to save time, but only if they are 100 per cent safe.

The order in which tricks are done will make a significant difference to the number of tricks which may be performed in twenty seconds. One way of saving time is to group together tricks which are performed on the

same wake so that less time is spent slaloming from wake to wake.

Practise tricks in short sequences of about four or more to see if they flow and if improvements can be made to one trick in order to finish in a good position to start the next.

Having decided on a run which is reasonably secure, try timing it to find out if further adjustments are required. Avoid rushing through the programme as one mistake will lose more time than if you progressed carefully. Finally, competition nerves tend to make you perform your tricks faster, so it is important to relax and take your time.

## JUMP

Familiarise yourself with the lake and conditions by watching other skiers. Good timing is important and every opportunity should be taken to observe the boat path and the approach to the ramp. Depending on the competition, you will be given either two or three jumps, so errors could be expensive. The first jump should be well measured to provide a good base from which to improve. A poor first jump means that you may have everything to do on the second – not a good situation to be in.

## Rerides

Rerides in jumping are given for the same reasons as in slalom, but the flags have different meanings. If the speed is too slow then it is deemed to be of disadvantage to the skier, and he or she is given the option to accept the score or take the jump again. If the speed is too fast then this assists the skier to go further and is an unfair advantage. The reride in this case is mandatory.

Another frequent source of rerides is due

*Fig 103   Keep your arms in and down for extra distance.*

to errors in measuring the distance of the jump. If the error is greater than 1.5m (1.5yd) and the distance shown is greater than any of the previous jumps, then the skier is entitled to take the jump again.

## SUMMARY

Success in competitive water skiing is due mainly to good preparation. An understand-ing of the principles involved and careful practice will ensure that you are ready for competition. Remember that in preparing for a competition it is important to do the same things as you would normally do in practice. For example, if you don't warm up in practice don't warm up for the competition. Try to keep every detail of your preparation the same.

# 11 Equipment

## CLOTHING

### Wet Suits

A good quality wet suit not only keeps you warm, but also offers some protection against falls. The main requirement is that it allows free movement around the shoulders and arms.

### Dry Suits

Excellent in winter but the warmth depends on the type of clothing underneath. Again, free movement around the arms and shoulders is important, but remember that the bulk of the suit increases the drag, especially on deep water starts.

### Life-Jackets

A good fitting life-jacket is essential and a worthwhile investment. Make sure that the front closes properly. A gap here will allow the full force of the water to hit your exposed chest. The jacket should also be long enough to give some protection to the kidneys and ideally should allow for free movement around the shoulders.

### Gloves

Gloves will give you extra grip, and are particularly useful for deep water starts on one ski and slalom skiing. They are essential if the handle is covered in oil.

## ROPE

The length of the rope varies depending on use. For jumping and barefoot the rope is 23m (25yd) long while for general purpose and slalom skiing it is 18.25m (19.95yd) long (although the slalom rope will have several shortening loops in it). The rope is made from nylon strands for strength and lightness when wet and should float. Avoid getting knots in the rope as this will affect its long-term durability.

## SKIS

A pair of skis suitable for beginners will be constructed from either wood or a combination of foam and fibreglass. The bottom is likely to be flat or slightly concave with wide tails. Skis with flat bottoms will be more stable in a straight line while the concave ones are far superior for cutting the wake. The ski to be used as a mono ski will have a rear toe strap and perhaps a larger fin on the bottom.

### Slalom Skis

These come in a great variety of shapes, sizes and flexibilities. The choice of ski will seriously affect your skiing so it is important to make the right decision. An honest appraisal of your level and the type of conditions prevalent where you ski will help in making the selection. If you have the opportunity to try a ski before buying, try your old ski first for a few runs before trying the

Fig 104   Combi pair.

new one. This is the only way to make an objective assessment of a ski and judge its true potential.

## Length

The length of a slalom ski may range between 160-180cm (63-70in) and the choice should take into account bodyweight and also the speed at which you ski. Below is a rough guide to making this choice.

## Shape

The shape of all skis is very similar – the main difference of note is in the width of the tail. A wider tail will give easier deep water starts but only at the expense of response during the turn.

## Bottom

There are a variety of different bottoms which are designed to work together with the edge, flexibility and rocker to give the desired performance (see Fig 106). Thus knowing whether the bottom is an 'edge-to-edge' or a 'tunnel' will not give much of a clue to the performance of the ski if taken on its own. The edges and texture of the bottom of the ski have a significant effect on performance and care should be taken to keep them in pristine condition by storing the ski in a protective bag or laying it on its side between sessions.

| Skier's Weight (kg/lb) | | Ski Size (cm/in) | |
|---|---|---|---|
| 36–45 (80–100) | 160 (63) | 160 (63) | – |
| 45–54 (100–120) | 165 (65) | 160 (63) | 160 (63) |
| 54–63 (120–140) | 165 (65) | 165 (65) | 160 (63) |
| 63–72 (140–160) | 170 (67) | 165 (65) | 165 (65) |
| 72–81 (160–180) | 170 (67) | 170 (67) | 165 (65) |
| 81–90 (180–200) | 175 (69) | 170 (67) | 170 (67) |
| 90+ (200+) | 175 (69) | 175 (69) | – |
| Boat Speed (kph/mph) | 49 (30) | 49–58 (30–36) | 58 (36) |

# Equipment

Fig 105   Notice that the front and rear bindings are close together. Ideally the toes of the rear foot should just be touching the front binding.

## Flexibility

The flex pattern of a ski is the most important factor determining its particular properties. Usually, the bottom of the ski can be divided into three areas. The area under the bindings is usually the stiffest as this is where the weight is. From the front binding to the front of the ski the flexibility softens, and the same is true of the flex approaching the tail of the ski. Generally, the flex at the front of the ski determines the rough water ability of the ski and that at the tail determines the turning ability.

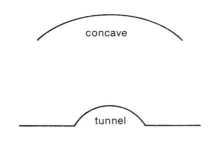

Fig 106   Types of bottom.

The softer the ski as a whole, the better its turning and rough water ability, making it a very forgiving ski. However, it is only if the ski is stiff that it will be fast since the edge design and rocker of stiff skis help to make the turns better. The drawback with the stiff ski is that it is generally less forgiving.

## Bindings

Bindings come in three types – adjustable, wrapped and high wrap – and they are ordered according to the degree of control they offer over the ski. Good support on the ankles is required for the best control.

The rear binding may be just a toe strap or a complete wrapped binding. The choice is up to you, but you should remember that the extra security of having double wrapped bindings is only purchased at the expense of a loss of flexibility in the knees, especially when crossing the wake.

**Binding placement**   The front and rear bindings should be placed as close as possible together. The toes of the rear foot should be just behind the front foot to allow maximum flexibility of the legs. The position of the front foot is very important as it affects the performance of the ski. By moving it forward, more of the ski rides in the water, making it accelerate and turn faster. However, if you move it too far forward it will pitch you over the front on the turn. Only small adjustments are required as a ski set up using manufacturers' instructions is correct for most skiers.

## Fins

In recent years a whole new generation of fins designed to optimise performance has appeared and the most important of these is the wing or foil fin. This works by presenting minimal drag when the ski is in its accelerating attitude and increased drag during the deceleration when more weight is put on the front foot. It improves deceleration and allows a better turn and better angle out of the turn.

Lateral adjustment is also becoming popular. However, although moving the fin towards the front improves the turn, the tail of the ski may jump out, while if you move the fin to the tail of the ski to assist in keeping the ski in the water, you do so at the expense of the turn.

By careful adjustment of fins and bindings the ski may be optimised for a particular use or style of skiing.

## Trick Skis

Trick skis are flat, short and wide. The edges may be square or rounded on the upper surface. Rounded edges help the skis turn by reducing the resistance to any spray hitting the side of the ski.

The bindings are placed so that the weight acts directly over the centre of the ski. The

Fig 107  Fin and wing.

binding for the single ski is slightly forward of the centre to compensate for the weight placed on the back of the ski when putting the foot in the back binding. The back binding is at an angle to make flexing the knees easier. The greater the angle the easier it is to flex the legs, but the harder it is to turn in the reverse direction.

The two shapes commonly encountered in trick skis are rounded ends and square ends. Round-end skis are easy to turn but offer less tracking so that cutting to the wake or gripping the water is difficult as there is less of a straight edge presented to the water. Square-end skis, it follows, are more suitable for wake tricks as they grip the water better, but are less easy to turn.

The stiffer the ski, the easier it is to turn and the easier it is to obtain lift from the wake. Stiff,

*Fig 108    The rear binding is offset to allow maximum flexibility of the legs.*

flat skis will ride higher in the water than soft skis and will therefore turn easier. Grooves in the bottom of the ski help with the tracking but reduce the ease with which the skis turn.

### Trick Rope

The handle for trick skiing has a toe strap incorporated for toe-hold tricks. This is usually made from a strong webbing covered with a soft, padded material. A good fit is essential as if it is too tight it will not come off and if it is too loose it will not stay on.

## Jump Skis

These are 165–190cm (65–75in) long and are constructed from wood or a combina-

tion of honeycomb and fibreglass. At the top end of the range skis made from honeycomb or a material like graphite or kevlar fibres (which increase the stiffness whilst remaining light) are available but expensive. The main criteria for choosing jump skis are stiffness, weight, length and expense. Stiff and light skis are the most expensive but are the most responsive. For all but the most advanced skiers a honeycomb and fibreglass ski is sufficient.

## Helmet

Safety dictates that you should have one. Make sure that the helmet gives protection to the ears and that the chin strap releases when pressure is applied.

# Appendix A

## Hand Signals

faster   turn around   speed ok   same speed

slower   back to the dock   I'm ok   stop

# Appendix B

## British Water Skiing Federation Grading Scheme

### Certificate of Merit

Issued to anyone who is able to ski.

### Bronze Grade

1. Unassisted dock start on two skis.
2. Unassisted deep water start on two skis.
3. Carry out connected virages across wakes.
4. Return to dock and whilst making a parallel approach to shore, release tow rope and make a safe and controlled landing.
5. Correct stance to be maintained throughout the test.

### Silver Grade

1. Dock start on two skis.
2. Deep water start on one ski.
3. Carry out connected virages across wake on mono ski, maintaining a correct position.
4. Return to dock and land in a controlled manner.

### Gold Grade

1. *Slalom* On mono ski make six continuous virages equally through both wakes within thirty seconds.
2. *Figures* On two trick skis complete the following:
   a) 180° turn, front-to-back
   b) 180° turn, back-to-front
   c) 360° turn, front-to-front
3. *Jumping* Complete one jump successfully.

The above grades may be tested by affiliated club secretaries, BWSF instructors and BWSF coaches. For all information on the sport, write to:

**British Water Ski Federation**
390 City Road
London EC1V 2QA

Telephone 01 833 2855

# Glossary

**Angle** Term used to indicate the angle through which the ski has turned.

**Arm sling** Device used on long-distance jumps to keep the pull from the boat at waist height as the skier leaves the ramp.

**Backwash** Rough water caused by other boats or waves reflected from solid objects (usually the shore).

**Binding** May be adjustable, fixed or high-wrap. Made from rubber and designed to allow the release of the foot after a fall.

**Boot binding** High-wrap binding giving maximum support.

**Combi pair** Pair of skis, one of which has been set up for use as a mono ski.

**Concave** A term used to describe the bottom of the ski. If the concave extends to the edge of the ski then it is called an 'edge-to-edge' concave. If the concave finishes before reaching the edge then it is called a 'tunnel' concave.

**Counter-cut** Cut used in jumping to get additional width.

**Crest** Top of wake.

**Crush** Collapsing with either the legs or body.

**Cut** Putting the ski on edge and crossing the wake.

**Edge** Keeping the ski on its edge.

**Entry gate** Used to signify the beginning of a course.

**Exit gate** Used to signify the end of a course.

**Fin** Gives directional stability to the ski.

**Flex** Usually applies to bending the knees to absorb the shock of hitting waves or the wake. The term is also used to describe the properties of the ski.

**Foil** Attached to the fin to increase deceleration.

**Lean** Leaning either towards or away from the boat to turn the ski.

**Line tricks** Tricks performed by turning and passing the foot over the rope.

**Mono** Single ski.

**Pre-turn** The initial part of the turn where the ski decelerates.

**Pull** Usually applies to using your body-weight to exert a force on the rope, but may also be used to indicate that the arms should be pulled in.

**Reach** Extending the arm towards the boat.

**Reride** In competition skiing, where the

# *Glossary*

pass has to be taken again because of an unfair advantage.

**Rocker**   The amount of permanent bend in the ski.

**Skegs**   The fins on the back of the ski.

**Skiing leg**   The front foot.

**Slalom**   Term given to a series of connected wake crossings.

**Surface tricks**   Tricks done on the water usually between the wakes.

**Table**   Flat surface of water between the two wakes.

**Toe hold**   Applies to the strap used to hold the foot in the handle and the tricks performed in this way.

**Tunnel**   *See* Concave

**Turning on axis**   The skier maintains balance while rotating around a fixed point.

**Virage**   Wake crossing.

**Wake tricks**   Tricks performed clear of the water using the wake to generate lift.

**Wing**   Same as foil.

**Whip**   Skiing wide of the boat as it turns to rapidly increase speed.

# Index

Angle
    related to lean   45
Aquaplaning   9

Bindings   102–3
Boat Path
    beginners   25
    jump   80, 84
    slalom   53

Counter-cut   88–90
Crossing the wake
    one ski   33–4
    two skis   21
Cut
    single wake   84
Cutting the wake   44

Deceleration   45–6
Deep water start
    one ski   34, 35
    two skis   14
Drop ski   34
Dry land lesson   12–17
Dry start
    one ski   39–40
    two skis   21–3
Dry suits   100

Edge   44
    change   45–6, 48
    crossing the wake   33, 34
    jump   86, 87
    tricks   63

Fin   103
Flat ski   44, 45
    jump   81, 84

Grip
    jump   80
    mono skiing   26, 32
    palms-down   12

Helmet   104

Injury   10

Jump start   39

Lean   33, 41–4, 48
    jump   81, 84
Life-jacket   100
    barefoot   91
    safety   17, 48
    tricks   60

Mental preparation   11

One-ski step off   91

Position
    jump   80
    one ski   31, 32
    one-ski start   34
    one-ski tricks   69
    toe holds   76
    two skis   17
    two-ski start   12, 19
    two-ski tricks   60, 63
Pre-turn   45–6, 52
Pull
    compensating for wind   58–9
    jump   84
    slalom   41–4, 52
    tricks   63
    wake tricks   65

Ramp   80, 81
Reaching   48–50, 52
Refusing
    jump   84, 86
Rerides   95–6, 98
Rope   100
    length   53, 57
    tricks   63, 104
    shortening   57
Rough water   58–9

# Index

Scooter start   37
Scoring   95
Ski
   bottom   101
   dropping   28–30
   flexibility   102
   jump   104
   length   101
   lifting   26
   shape   101
   slalom   100–3
   tricks   103–4
Skiing leg   26
Slack rope
   during turn   49, 52
   one-ski dry start   40
   scooter start   37
   two-ski dry start   23
   two skis   26
Slalom course   53–4
   entry gate   53, 55–7, 95
   exit gate   53
Speed
   barefoot   91
   beginners   25
   during turn   45
   jump   80, 84
   slalom course   53
   tricks   63

Spray   32
Step over   75–6

Three-quarter cut   87
Toe holds   76, 79
Trick
   programme   60, 96–8
   scoring   98
Turn   47, 52
   initiating, toe hold   76–9
   initiating, tricks   63, 64
   rate of   46, 50

Upper body   44
   movement   14
   strong   32, 34
   tricks   63

Wake tricks   65–71
   generating lift   68
Warming up   10–11
Weight distribution   31–2
   crossing the wake   33
   during turn   46, 47, 48, 49–50
   jump   80, 84
   one-ski tricks   69
   two-ski tricks   63
Wet suits   100
Wing   103

# Other Titles in The Skills of the Game Series

| | | |
|---|---|---|
| * | **American Football** | Les Wilson |
| * | **Badminton** | Peter Roper |
| * | **Basketball** | Paul Stimpson |
| * | **Canoeing** | Neil Shave |
| * | **Cricket** | Keith Andrew |
| | **Cross-Country Skiing** | Paddy Field & Tim Walker |
| * | **Crown Green Bowls** | Harry Barratt |
| * | **Endurance Running** | Norman Brook |
| * | **Fitness for Sport** | Rex Hazeldine |
| * | **Golf** | John Stirling |
| * | **Hockey** | John Cadman |
| * | **Judo** | Tony Reay |
| | **Jumping** | Malcolm Arnold |
| * | **Karate** | Vic Charles |
| | **Orienteering** | Carol McNeill |
| | **Rhythmic Gymnastics** | Jenny Bott |
| | **Rugby League** | Maurice Bamford |
| * | **Rugby Union** | Barrie Corless |
| * | **Sprinting and Hurdling** | Peter Warden |
| * | **Skiing** | John Shedden |
| * | **Squash** | Ian McKenzie |
| * | **Swimming** | John Verrier |
| * | **Table Tennis** | Gordon Steggall |
| * | **Tennis** | Charles Applewhaite & Bill Moss |
| | **Throwing** | Max Jones |
| | **Triathlon** | Steve Trew |
| * | **Volleyball** | Keith Nicholls |
| * | **Windsurfing** | Ben Oakley |

* **Also available in paperback**

Further details of titles available or in preparation can be obtained from the publishers.